The **Goodbye** *Book*

The Goodbye Book

Robert Ramsay & Randall Toye

A Jonathan-James Book

PADDINGTON PRESS LTD

NEW YORK & LONDON

ISBN 0 7092 0688 7

Printed and bound in the United States of America

Jonathan-James Books
5 Sultan Street
Toronto, Ontario
Canada M5S 1L6

Illustrations by David Shaw
Designed by Jack Steiner
Edited by Randall Toye

IN THE UNITED KINGDOM
PADDINGTON PRESS

IN SOUTHERN AFRICA
Distributed by
ERNEST STANTON (PUBLISHERS) (PTY) LTD

IN AUSTRALIA AND NEW ZEALAND
Distributed by
A.H. & A.W. REED

To Maureen and Helga
R.R.

To Claudia and Gary
R.T.

Contents

Foreword

Dr. Johnson sagely observed that "a man will turn over half a library to make a book," which is what we have done in bringing together this collection of goodbyes. We do not make any claim that our work is complete or even exhaustive. It merely scratches a surface where a certain need for scratching made itself felt. We have no doubt that many readers will think of dozens of memorable goodbye scenes that have, for one reason or another, eluded us. They are welcome to turn over the other half of Dr. Johnson's library.

A book comprised of endings hardly seems to call for a Foreword, but it is satisfying to reflect a little on the nature of goodbyes. Farewelling has obtained the status of a sub-genre in the study of literature and life. It seems that nothing becomes some people as taking leave of a lover, a dear friend, a political position or life itself. Why this is so raises two questions that beg answering: how does one deliver an eloquent goodbye, and what do goodbyes mean?

An answer to the first question centers around a human fondness for beginnings, middles and ends. Pessimists resist and say that life is not quite so neat and that we are naive to think so, but most of us choose to ignore such advice and strive to order our existence and to make life easier. Goodbyes help to achieve order in the sense that they conclude a love affair, a journey, a career or a life. The chaos of change eventually subsides and life always goes on. Perhaps because goodbyes are often premeditated, they are usually well worded, but always to the point.

As to what goodbyes mean, we believe they are but one of the celebrated rites of passage through life. Shirley MacLaine once said that "the pain of leaving those you grow to love is only the prelude to understanding yourself and others." And since saying goodbye is increasingly as much a part of life as saying hello, it is well to learn the art of leavetaking with grace, wit and charm. *The Goodbye Book* is a guide to saying goodbye in every kind of situation as represented through history.

Part One of this book deals almost exclusively with goodbyes between lovers in film, poetry, plays and letters. Some will cause you to weep, and some are sure to inspire — all are beautifully eloquent. We have consulted a number of standard collections of love poetry and love letters, and we wish to thank all of those who have made our task somewhat lighter.

Part Two illustrates the many ways that political figures have said farewell. Politicians are infamous for their goodbyes, and history shall no doubt justly bestow the farewelling crown upon Richard Nixon. We had thought that the politician's high profile would bring their demise a good deal of attention. Sadly, such is not the case and we have had to rummage through many a newspaper clipping file to arrive at the few included here. We apologize for the countless number we may have overlooked.

Part Three is given to last words, a subject that has interested a number of collectors before us. The work Edward Le Comte in his *Dictionary of Last Words* and Barnaby Conrad in his *Famous Last Words* were invaluable.

If somewhat morbid, collecting last words is a fascinating pastime. Goodbyes from the gallows, like the scaffold letters, are haunting eyewitness accounts of history. Few people ever have sufficient time to compose their last words in a manner they would find wholly suitable. For example, there is a famous parody of last words in *Peter Pan* where Captain Hook makes his dying speech prematurely "lest when dying there be no time for it."

Goodbyes often account for some of our most intense moments in life and, as such, are not deserving of the relative obscurity which they have been accorded. It is our hope that *The Goodbye Book* will go some way towards putting goodbyes in their proper place among the ways we express ourselves. You may even find some scope for *The Goodbye Book* in playing those favorite parlor games, Unrecorded Last Words and Unwritten Farewell Letters. For as Cleopatra may have written to Mark Antony:

> Dear Mark — What a wonderful time I had sailing this afternoon. I am just going off to feed the snakes and shall look for you when you arrive. Love, Cleo.

Robert Ramsay and Randall Toye
Toronto, 1979.

The **Goodbye** *Book*

Part One

Here's looking at you, kid.

Chapter 1

"Come let us kiss and part."

Michael Drayton

" 'Tis better to have loved and lost, than never to have loved at all," lamented the poet Alfred Lord Tennyson. And if the history of romance is filled with beautiful and lyrical declarations of love, it is equally complete with eloquent and often heart-rending goodbyes. Poets, letter writers, playwrights, novelists and film makers have all given voice to the lover's farewell; it is a voice that carries from the sad to the humorous, and from the poignant to the thankful.

The frequency with which lovers part has spawned a literature of its own. Writers from Shakespeare to Byron, from George Eliot to Kahlil Gibran have all made observations on the subject of parting, and their comments reflect centuries of farewelling.

Saying goodbye to someone that you once loved is as much a part of life as saying hello. It is an unhappy truth to which Samuel Taylor Coleridge paid service:

> *To meet, to know, to love — and then to part,*
> *Is the sad tale of many a human heart.*

Bryon Forceythe Willson took a similarly pragmatic, if unhappy, view of the situation:

> *We live to love; we meet to part;*
> *And part to meet on earth no more.*

While Edward Young, with a bow to forces beyond our control, summed it up in one line:

> *But Fate ordains that dear friends must part.*

Having resolved to say goodbye, the question arises as to how the farewell should be most tactfully handled. While many might choose to linger long in hopes of recantation and reconcliation, greater minds have counselled to cut your losses and retire. Shakespeare was of the opinion that farewells were not something to dally over:

> *Let us not be dainty of leave-taking,*
> *But shift away.*

Lord Byron held a similar view:

> *All farewells should be sudden, when forever.*

And Elizabeth Asquith Bebesco echoed both sentiments:

> *It is never any good dwelling on good-byes. It*
> *is not the being together that it prolongs, it*
> *is the parting.*

Other contributors to the literature of parting have suggested a myriad of ways of viewing the final farewell. Saying goodbye can be an experience of self-discovery:

> *The pain of leaving those you grow to love is*
> *only the prelude to understanding yourself and*
> *others.*
>
> Shirley MacLaine

Or it can teach expediency:

> *It's better to learn to say good-bye early than late.*
>
> Jessamyn West

It can show you the extent of love:

> *Only in the agony of parting do we look into the depths of love.*
>
> George Eliot

> *Ever has it been that love knows not its own depth until the hour of*
> *separation.*
>
> Kahlil Gibran

And it can be an expression of regret:

> *You leave me much against my will.*
>
> Edna St. Vincent Millay

> *It's not love's going hurts my days,*
> *But that it went in little ways.*
>
> Edna St. Vincent Millay

Ernest Hemingway reflected that "If two people love each other there can be no happy end to it." And the pain of parting has inspired many poetic comments on the nature of farewells:

> *How shall you speak of parting?*
> *How shall the bonds be loosened*
> *That friendship fastened round you?*
>
> Madeline Mason-Manheim

> *Please understand the heart of one who leaves as the water in the*
> *streams; never to return again.*
>
> Princess Kazu-no-miya

*There's a kind of release
And a kind of torment in every good-bye
   for every man.*

C. Day-Lewis

In the popular song, *Did You Ever Have To Make Up Your Mind?*, John Sebastian suggested that ultimately you have to go with one and leave the other behind. For the person who leaves, the pain of parting is often lessened by the excitement of a new relationship. But for those left behind, parting can leave a gaping hole in life:

Sometimes, when one person is missing, the whole world seems depopulated.

Lamartine

*Feel not the pain of parting.
It is those who stay behind that suffer.*

Longfellow

*The one who goes is happier
Than those he leaves behind.*

Edward Pollock

Thou art gone from my gaze like a beautiful dream.

George Linley

Every thought of her goes through me like a spear!

John Keats, referring to Fanny Brawne.

Yet on occasion the person taking leave feels an equal sorrow:

Good-byes breed a sort of distaste for whomever you say good-bye to; this hurts, you feel, this must not happen again.

Elizabeth Bowen

*Going away: I can generally bear the separation,
but I don't like the leave taking.*

Samuel Butler

The metaphysical poets of the seventeenth century often couched the act of making love in an image of death, responding to the belief that sexual intercourse shortened one's life. But the theme of death also finds expression in the literature of parting:

*Partir c'est mourir un peu:
To part is to die a little.*

French proverb

*To leave is to die a little,
To die to what we love.
We leave behind a bit of ourselves
Wherever we have been.*

Edmond Haraucourt

In every parting there is an image of death.

George Eliot

Their meetings made December June,
Their every parting was to die.

Alfred Lord Tennyson

Alfred Lord Tennyson

Every parting gives a foretaste of death.

Schopenhauer

When I died last, and dear, I die
As often as from thee I go.

John Donne

There is death in a true friend's farewell.

Marceline Desbordes-Valmore

Together they can long endure,
Yet once they are separated
The Hazel dies almost at once,
The honeysuckle very soon.
My darling, it is so with us:
No you sans, no me sans you.

Marie de France

Parting is worse than death; it is the death of love.

John Dryden

Poetry is a vast reservoir of emotions, not all of which appear to be happily recollected in tranquility. Goodbye poetry in particular displays an urgency of feeling that has an immediacy regardless of when it was written. Emily Dickinson's *Parting* continues the death-in-parting theme, ambiguously casting it as both heavenly and hellish:

PARTING

My life closed twice before its close;
  It yet remains to see
If Immortality unveil
  A third event to me,

So huge, so hopeless to conceive,
  As these that twice befell:
Parting is all we know of heaven,
  And all we need of hell.

Emily Dickinson

Sir Philip Sidney's *Sonnet* echoes the sentiment that parting is a living death, extracting all the best in life and leaving only the worst:

SONNET

Oft have I mused, but now at length I find,
  Why those that die, men say they do depart:
Depart, a word so gentle to my mind,
  Weakly did seem to paint death's ugly dart.

But now the stars with their strange course do bind
  Me one to leave, with whom I leave my heart.
I hear a cry of spirits faint and blind,
  That parting thus my chiefest part I part.

Part of my life, the loathed part to me,
  Lives to impart my weary clay some breath.
But that good part, wherein all comforts be,
  Now dead, doth shew departure is a death.
    Yea worse than death, death parts both woe and joy,
    From joy I part still living in annoy.

Sir Philip Sidney

I shall die a little! It is a melancholy assessment of parting. But, *non omnis moriar,* I shall not completely die. In fact, some observers of life have wondered what all of the fuss is about:

Why should we hesitate to say "good-by" to each other? Are we not Pagans to think that a word has power over God's quiet purposes, and that saying "good-by" smells of death?

Maltbie Babcock

The happy never say, and never hear said, farewell.
Walter Savage Landor

And there is always the possibility of a reconciliation, in which case:

The return makes one love the farewell.
Alfred de Musset

However, it may well be that no reconciliation is desired:

> *Some weep because they part,*
> *And languish broken-hearted.*
> *And others — O my heart! —*
> *Because they never parted.*

Thomas Baily Aldrich

Absence makes the heart grow fonder — of somebody else.
Anonymous

Ending an affair has been known to be a pretty sticky business, and there is a certain irony in the fact that many lovers part on the same note as they met — with a kiss:

> *Kiss me, and say good-bye;*
> *Good-bye, there is no word to say but this.*

Andrew Lang

> *Now, in the summit of love's topmost peak,*
> *Kiss and we part; no farther can we go.*

Aldred Austin

> *And lips to lips! Yet once more ere we part,*
> *Clasp me and make me thine, as mine thou art.*

Robert Browning

Robert Dodsley's poem on this subject is still capable of finding an audience today. As an expression of goodbye, *The Parting Kiss* is both poignant and lyrical:

THE PARTING KISS

One kind kiss before we part,
Drop a tear, and bid adieu:
Though we sever, my fond heart
Till we meet shall pant for you.

Yet, yet, weep not so, my love,
Let me kiss that falling tear.
Though my body must remove,
All my soul will still be here.

All my soul and all my heart,
And every wish shall pant for you;
One kind kiss then ere we part,
Drop a tear and bid adieu.

Robert Dodsley

Michael Drayton's justly famous sonnet, *The Parting*, differs from other poems on the kissing and parting theme in its exclusion of the traditional plea for reconciliation. The speaker in Drayton's poem appears to have been wronged once too often, and is now happy to say goodbye and maintain a measure of self-respect:

THE PARTING

Since there's no help, come let us kiss and part,
Nay, I have done: you get no more of me,
And I am glad, yea, glad with all my heart,
That thus so cleanly I myself can free,
Shake hands for ever, cancel all our vows,
And when we meet at any time again,
Be it not seen in either of our brows,
That we one jot of former love retain;
Now at the last gasp, of love's latest breath,
When, his pulse failing, passion speechless lies,
When faith is kneeling by his bed of death,
And innocence is closing up his eyes,
  Now if thou would'st, when all have given him over,
  From death to life, thou might'st him yet recover.

Michael Drayton

Robert Burns' *Farewell to Nancy* is among the most famous of all poems celebrating the parting kiss, and one of the most well known goodbye poems of all time. It contains all the elements of the classic goodbye — unrequited love, despair, hope, good wishes and a plea to be remembered down the years:

FAREWELL TO NANCY

Ae fond kiss, and then we sever;
Ae fareweel, and then for ever!
Deep in heart-wrung tears I'll pledge thee,
Warring sighs and groans I'll wage thee. —

Who shall say that Fortune grieves him,
While the star of hope she leaves him:
Me, nae chearful twinkle lights me;
Dark despair around benights me. —

I'll ne'er blame my partial fancy,
Naething could resist my Nancy:
But to see her, was to lover her;
Love but her, and love for ever. —

Had we never lov'd sae kindly,
Had we never lov'd sae blindly!
Never met — or never parted,
We had ne'er been broken-hearted.

Fare-thee-weel, thou first and fairest!
Fare-thee-weel, thou best and dearest!
Thine be ilka joy and treasure,
Peace, Enjoyment, Love and Pleasure! —

Ae fond kiss, and then we sever!
Ae fareweel, Alas, for ever!
Deep in heart-wrung tears I'll pledge thee,
Warring sighs and groans I'll wage thee. —

Robert Burns

ROBBIE
BURNS

Others cannot bear the thought of a parting kiss that would flood them with tender memories of remembered happiness. William Shakespeare's song, *Take, O take those lips away* from *Measure for Measure* expresses all of the delicate sadness of saying goodbye:

TAKE, O TAKE THOSE LIPS AWAY

Take, O take those lips away,
  That so sweetly were forsworn,;
And those eyes, the break of day,

Lights that do mislead the morn:
But my kisses bring again, bring again.
Seals of love, but seal'd in vain, seal'd in vain.

William Shakespeare

The bitter feelings of a betrayed lover are the subject of Sir Thomas Wyatt's *A Revocation.* It is a poem filled with reproach, and Wyatt plays on the tradition of the parting kiss by having his speaker depart unkissed:

A REVOCATION

What should I say,
   Since Faith is dead,
And Truth away
   From you is fled?
   Should I be led
     With doubleness?
     Nay, nay, mistress!

I promised you
   And you promised me,
To be as true,
   As I would be.
   But since I see
     Your double heart,
     Farewell my part!

Thought for to take
   'Tis not my mind;
But to forsake
   One so unkind;
   And as I find
     So will I trust.
     Farewell, unjust!

Can ye say nay,
   But that you said
That I alway
   Should be obeyed?
   And — thus betrayed,
     Ere that I wist,
     Farewell, unkist!

Sir Thomas Wyatt

If you are not up for kissing, and not everyone is when they are saying goodbye, you may choose to part with no more than a final word. This word, like a locket of remembrance, becomes a symbol of an entire relationship. Thomas Otway's request appears more than a little cloying:

If we must part forever,
Give me but one kind word to think upon,
And please myself withal, whilst my heart is breaking.

While Jean Paul Richter is staidly philosophical:

Never part without loving words to think of during your absence. It
may be that you will not meet again in life.

And Lord Byron, who as we have seen believes that all goodbyes should be sudden, judiciously decides upon a single word:

Farewell! A word that must be, and hath been —
A sound which makes us linger; — yet — Farewell!

Personally, it would seem that a good solid arguement is one of the finest ways to end an affair. But poets have a way of elevating all sentiments to the highest degree of delicacy, and there can be little delicacy in an argument. So you might opt instead to say goodbye in silent sorrow. Ernest Dowson seemed to have this theme uppermost in his mind when he composed the following two poems, where the value of silence outstrips the value of language:

O MORS! QUAM AMARA EST
MEMORIA TUA HOMINI PACEM
HABENTI IN SUBSTANTIIS SUIS

Exceeding sorrow
  Consumeth my sad heart!
Because to-morrow
  We must depart,
Now is exceeding sorrow
  All my part!

Give over playing,
  Cast thy viol away:
Merely laying
  Thine head my way:
Prithee, give over playing,
  Grave or gay.

Be no word spoken,
  Weep nothing: let a pale
Silence, unbroken
  Silence, prevail!
Prithee, be no word spoken,
  Lest I fail!

Forget to-morrow.
Weep nothing: only lay
In silent sorrow
Thine head my way:
Let us forget to-morrow,
This one day!

Ernest Dowson

A VALEDICTION

If we must part,
Then let it be like this;
Not heart on heart,
Nor with the useless anguish of a kiss;
But touch mine hand and say;
'Until tomorrow or some other day,
If we must part.'

Words are so weak
When love hath been so strong:
Let silence speak:

'Life is a little while, and love is long;
A time to sow and reap,
And after harvest a long time to sleep,
But words are weak.'

Ernest Dowson

Half the promises never kept were never made, but you are unlikely to convince a wronged lover of that. Shakespeare recognized it:

SONNET CXXXVIII

When my love swears that she is made of truth,
I do believe her, though I know she lies.

And Dorothy Parker updated the sentiment:

UNFORTUNATE COINCIDENCE

By the time you swear you're his,
Shivering and sighing,
And he vows his passion is
Infinite, undying —
Lady make note of this:
One of you is lying.

The greatest promise that a lover can make is for fidelity, and it is the promise most often made and most often broken. From fidelity to inconstancy is all too often too short a journey and, next to marriage, love's inconstancy elicits more farewells than any other activity. The object of affection is chased, caught, prized and cast unceremoniously aside. Sir

William Shakespeare & Dorothy Parker — A Chance Encounter

Thomas Wyatt's *Farewell, all my welfare* captures all the remorse of the
spurned lover as he refelcts on his fate:

FAREWELL, ALL MY WELFARE

Farewell, all my welfare,
My shoe is trod awry;
Now I may cark and care
To sing lullay by by.
Alas, what shall I do thereto?
There is no shift to help me now.

Who made it such offence
To love for love again?
God wot that my pretence
Was but to ease his pain;
For I had ruth to see his woe.
Alas, more fool, why did I so?

For he from me is gone
And makes thereat a game,
And hath left me alone
To suffer sorrow and shame.
Alas, he is unkind and doubtless
To leave me thus all comfortless.

It is a grievous smart
To suffer pains and sorrow;
But most it grieved my heart
He laid his faith to borrow:
And falsehood hath his faith and truth,
And he forsworn by many an oath.

All ye lovers, perdy,
Have cause to blame his deed,
Which shall example be
To let you off your speed;
Let never woman again
Trust to such words as men can fain.

For I, unto my cost,
Am warning to you all
That they whom you trust most
Soonest deceive you shall;
But, complaint cannot redress
Of my great grief the great excess.

Sir Thomas Wyatt

Walter Savage Landor was no less poetic and correct when he came to write about the fickleness of love:

SONG

O fond, but fickle and untrue,
Ianthe take my last adieu.
Your heart one day will ask you why
You forced from me this farewell sigh.
Have you not feign'd that friends reprove
The mask of Frendship worn by Love?
Feign'd, that they whisper'd you should be
The same to others as to me?
Ah! little knew they what they said!
How would they blush to be obey'd!
   Too swiftly roll'd the wheels when last
These woods and airy downs we past.
Fain would we trace the winding path,
And hardly wisht for blissful Bath.
At every spring you caught my arm,
And every pebble roll'd alarm.
On me was turn'd that face divine,
The view was on the right so fine:
I smiled .. those conscious eyes withdrew ..
The left was now the finer view.
Each trembled for detected wiles,
And blushes tinged our fading smiles.

But Love turns Terror into jest . .
We laught, we kist, and we confest.
Laugh, kisses, confidence are past,
And Love goes too . . but goes the last.

Walter Savage Landor

John Wilmot's mistress was fond of dispensing her favours so lightly and so freely that he saw no other course but to say goodbye:

UPON HIS LEAVING HIS MISTRESS

'Tis not that I am weary grown
Of being yours, and yours alone;
But with what face can I incline
To damn you to be only mine?
   You, whom some kinder power did fashion,
   By merit and by inclination,
   The joy at least of one whole nation.

Let meaner spirits of your sex
With humbler aims their thoughts perplex,
And boast if by their arts they can
Contrive to make one *happy man;*
   Whilst, moved by an impartial sense,
   Favours like nature you dispense
   With universal influence.

See, the kind seed-receiving earth
To every grain affords a birth.
On her no showers unwelcome fall;
Her willing womb retains 'em all.
   And shall my Celia be confined?
   No! Live up to thy mighty mind,
   And be the mistress of mankind.

John Wilmot, Earl of Rochester

Not all of us, however, possess Wilmot's charming flair for the picaresque. Indeed, there is a well-known class of lovers who have been justly rebuked for giving romance a bad name; they have often been described as the "clinging vines". It is the lot of these unfortunate souls to forever love not wisely but too well, and they invariably encounter great difficulties in saying goodbye. In *I will not let thee go*, Robert Bridges brutally personifies this personality, while A. E. Housman treats him with a little more kindness:

I WILL NOT LET THEE GO

I will not let thee go.
I hold thee by too many bands:
Thou sayest farewell, and lo!
I have thee by the hands,
And will not let thee go.

Robert Bridges

BECAUSE I LIKED YOU BETTER

Because I liked you better
  Than suits a man to say,
It irked you, and I promised
  To throw the thought away.

To put the world between us
  We parted, stiff and dry;
'Good-bye', said you, 'forget me.'
  'I will, no fear', said I.

If here, where clover whitens
  The dead man's knoll, you pass,
And no tall flower to meet you
  Starts in the trefoiled grass,

Halt by the headstone naming
  The heart no longer stirred,
And say the lad that loved you
  Was one that kept his word.

A. E. Housman

In succeeding generations the act of war has played an equally important role in contributing to goodbye literature. In time of war the first casualty may be truth but as the following poems illustrate, the second is surely love:

GOOD-BYE DOLLY GRAY

Good-bye Dolly; I must leave you,
Though it breaks my heart to go;
Something tells me that I'm needed
At the front to fight the foe.

Will D. Cobb

GOING TO THE WARS
  (To Lucasta)

Tell me not, Sweet, I am unkind,
  That from the nunnery
Of thy chaste breast, and quiet mind,
  To war and arms I fly.

True, a new mistress now I chase,
  The first foe in the field;
And with a stronger faith embrace
  A sword, a horse, a shield.

Yet this inconstancy is such
  As you too shall adore;
I could not love thee, Dear, so much,
Lov'd I not honour more.

Richard Lovelace

Where Cobb and Lovelace strike the note of honor for one's country over that of love, the Welsh poet Alun Lewis sounds a more personal and intimate chord in his war poem, *Goodbye:*

GOODBYE

So we must say Goodbye, my darling,
And go, as lovers go, for ever;
Tonight remains, to pack and fix on labels
And make an end of lying down together.

I put a final shilling in the gas,
And watch you slip your dress below your knees
And lie so still I hear your rustling comb
Modulate the autumn in the trees.

And all the countless things I shall remember
Lay mummy-cloths of silence round my head;
I fill the carafe with a drink of water;
You say, 'We paid a guinea for this bed,'

And then, 'We'll leave some gas, a little warmth
For the next resident, and these dry flowers,'
And turn your face away, afraid to speak
The big word, that Eternity is ours.

Your kisses close my eyes and yet you stare
As though God struck a child with nameless fears;
Perhaps the water glitters and discloses
Time's chalice and its limpid useless tears.

Everything we renounce except ourselves;
Selfishness is the last of all to go;
Our sighs are exhalations of the earth,
Our footprints leave a track across the snow.

We made the universe to be our home,
Our nostrils took the wind to be our breath,
Our hearts are massive towers of delight,
We stride across the seven seas of death.

Yet when all's done you'll keep the emerald
I placed upon your finger in the street;
And I will keep the patches that you sewed
On my old battledress tonight, my sweet.

Alun Lewis

If war holds within itself the prospect of death, and so goodbye forever, suicide is an equally devastating war with one's self. Fanny Godwin, whose touching suicide note appears in Part Three of this book, took her own life. Her death elicited the following goodbye from the Romantic poet Percy Bysshe Shelley:

ON FANNY GODWIN

Her voice did quiver as we parted,
Yet knew I not that heart was broken
From which it came, and I departed
Heeding not the words then spoken.
Misery — O Misery,
This world is all too wide for thee.

Percy Bysshe Shelley

Another Romantic poet, George Gordon, Lord Byron, penned more goodbye scenes than any other poet in the English language. So numerous are Byron's farewells that Bert Leston Taylor wrote of him:

"Farewell!" Into the lover's soul
you see fate plunge the fatal iron.
All poets use it. It's the whole
Of Byron.
"I only feel — Farewell!" said he;
And always fearful was the telling —
Lord Byron was eternally
Farewelling.

The following two poems are vintage Byron, displaying the pain, the sorrow, the fruitless hope and the finality of a lover's goodbye:

WHEN WE TWO PARTED

When we two parted
In silence and tears,
Half broken-hearted
To sever for years,
Pale grew they cheek and cold,
Colder thy kiss;
Truly that hour foretold
Sorrow to this.

The dew of the morning
  Sunk chill on my brow —
It felt like the warning
  Of what I feel now.
Thy vows are all broken,
  And light is thy fame:
I hear thy name spoken,
  And share in its shame.

They name thee before me,
  A knell to mine ear;
A shudder comes o'er me —
  Why wert thou so dear?
They know not I knew thee,
  Who knew thee to well:
Long, long shall I rue thee,
  Too deeply, to tell.

In secret we met —
  In silence I grieve,
That thy heart could forget,
  Thy spirit deceive.
  If I should meet thee
  After long years,
How should I greet thee?
  With silence and tears.

Lord Byron

FAREWELL!

Farewell! if ever fondest prayer
  For other's weal availed on high,
Mine will not all be lost in air,
  But waft thy name beyond the sky.
'Twere vain to speak, to weep, to sigh:
  Oh! more than tears of blood can tell,
When wrung from guilt's expiring eye,
  Are in that word — Farewell! — Farewell!

These lips are mute, these eyes are dry;
  But in my breast and in my brain,
Awake the pangs that pass not by,
  The thought that ne'er shall sleep again.
My soul nor deigns nor dares complain,
  Though grief and passion there rebel;
I only know we loved in vain —
  I only feel — Farewell! — Farewell!

Lord Byron

A lover is a practitioner of self-delusion, though you will go further as a lover if you are able to delude others as well. And nowhere is self-delusion more in evidence than when it comes time to say goodbye, when it usually masquerades as hope. Hope is reputed to spring eternal in the human breast, and discarded lovers apply it to their wounded hearts like salve to a skinned knee. In the following poems, Harold Monro's speaker reminds one of nothing so much as a puppy left out in the rain, while Coventry Patmore graces his hopeful lover with more worldly ways:

A FAREWELL

With all my will, but much against my heart,
We two now part.
My Very Dear,
Our solace is, the sad road lies so clear.
It needs no art,
With faint, averted feet
And many a tear,
In our opposed paths to persevere.
Go thou to East, I West.
We will not say
There's any hope, it is so far away.
But, O, my Best,
When the one darling of our widowhead,
The nursling Grief,
Is dead,
And no dews blur our eyes
To see the peach-bloom come in evening skies,
Perchance we may,
Where now this night is day,
And even through faith of still averted feet,
Making full circle of our banishment,
Amazed meet;
The bitter journey to the bourne so sweet
Seasoning the termless feast of our content
With tears of recognition never dry.

Coventry Patmore

THE TERRIBLE DOOR

Too long outside your door I have shivered.
You open it? I will not stay.
I'm haunted by your ashen beauty.
Take back your hand. I have gone away.

Don't talk, but move to that near corner.
I loathe the long cold shadow here.
We will stand a moment in the lamplight,
Until I watch you hard and near.

Happy release! Good-bye for ever!
Here at the corner we say good-bye.
But if you want me, if you do need me,
Who waits, at the terrible door, but I?

Harold Monro

For reasons which we are certain are known only to them, rejected lovers who hold out hope of reconciliation have an unaccountable desire to be heard saying, "well, if we can't be lovers, and I don't know why you say we can't be, let's at least be friends." This alone should provide ample evidence that there is no fool like a fool in love. Robert Browning's *The Lost Mistress* sums up the feelings of such a relationship. The final stanza is perfect in its expression of a lover reduced to the status of a friend:

THE LOST MISTRESS

All's over, then: does truth sound bitter
As one at first believes?
Hark, 'tis the sparrows' good-night twitter
About your cottage eaves!

And the leaf-buds on the vine are woolly,
I noticed that, today;
One day more bursts them open fully
— You know the red turns grey.

Tomorrow we meet the same then, dearest?
May I take your hand in mine?
Mere friends are we, — friends the merest
Keep much that I resign:

For each glance of the eye so bright and black,
Though I keep with heart's endeavour, —
Your voice, when you wish the snowdrops back,
Though it stay in my soul for ever! —

Yet I will but say what mere friends say,
Or only a thought stronger;
I will hold your hand but as long as all may,
Or so very little longer!

Robert Browning

Fortunately, ex-lovers do not make very good friends. When an affair has run its course, and kisses are made from habit rather than for pleasure, there is little left to say but goodbye. As Elinor Wylie sagely observes in *Felo De Se,* it is a time to unlearn to love:

FELO DE SE

My heart's delight, I must for love forget you;
I must put you from my heart, the better to please you;
I must make the power of the spirit set you
Beyond the power of the mind to seize you.

My dearest heart, in this last act of homage,
I must reject you; I must unlearn to love you;
I must make my eyes give up your adorable image
And from the inner chamber of my soul remove you.

Heart of my heart, the heart alone has courage
Thus to relinquish; it is yourself that stills you
In all my pulses, and dissolves the marriage
Of soul and soul, and at the heart's core kills you.

Elinor Wylie

Ben Jonson compares the lover's goodbye to the sun being forced from the sky, with total darkness enveloping all:

AN ELEGY

Since you must go, and I must bid farewell,
   Hear, Mistress, your departing servant tell
What it is like, and do not think they can
   Be idle words, though of a parting man.
It is as if a night should shade noonday,
   Or that the sun was here, but forc'd away,
And we were left under that hemisphere
   Where we must feel it dark for half a year.
What fate is this, to change men's days and hours,
   To shift their seasons, and destroy their powers!
Alas, I have lost my heat, my blood, my prime —
   Winter is come a quarter ere his time,
My health will leave me; and when you depart,
   How shall I do, sweet Mistress, for my heart?
You would restore it? No, that's worth a fear,
   As if it were not worthy to be there;
Oh, keep it still, for it had rather be
Your sacrifice than here remain with me,
And so I spare it. Come what can become
   Of me, I'll softly tread unto my tomb,
Or like a ghost walk silent amongst men,
   Till I may see both it and you again.

Ben Jonson

Algernon Charles Swinburne's short poem,*An Interlude,* is more cavalier in its approach to the goodbye:

AN INTERLUDE

I remember the way we parted,
The day and the way we met;
You hoped we were both broken-hearted;
And knew we should both forget.

Algernon Charles Swinburne

Edward Thomas was not so cavalier, but given his choice of imagery he does the best he can. If she was "like the touch of rain," he was certainly all wet:

LIKE THE TOUCH OF RAIN

Like the touch of rain she was
On a man's flesh and hair and eyes
When the joy of walking thus
Has taken him by surprise:

With the love of the storm he burns,
He sings, he laughs, well I know how,
But forgets when he returns
As I shall not forget her 'Go now'.

Those two words shut a door
Between me and the blessed rain
That was never shut before
And will not open again.

Edward Thomas

Francis Thompson's *Daisy* says it all about the act of saying goodbye:

DAISY

She went her unremembering way,
She went and left in me
The pang of all the partings gone,
And partings yet to be.

Francis Thompson

And Alexander Scott casts the discarded lover in the role of the unhappy wanderer, woeful and piteous, and capable of but one love:

LAMENT OF THE MASTER OF ERSKINE

Depairt, depairt, depairt,
Alas! I must depairt
From her that has my hairt,
With hairt full sore,
Aganis my will indeed,
And can find no remeid:
I wait the pains of deid
Can do no more.

Now must I go, alas!
From sicht of her sweet face,
The ground of all my grace,
*   And sovereign;*
What chance that may fall me,
Sall I never merry be,
Unto the time I see
*   My sweet again.*

I go, and wat not where,
I wander here and there,
I weep and sichis sair
*   With painis smart;*
Now must I pass away, away,
In wilderness and wilsome way,
Alas! this woeful day
*   We suld depairt!*

My spreit does quake for dread,
My thirlit hairt does bleed,
My painis does exceed —
*   What suld I say?*
I, woeful wicht, alone,
Makand ane piteous moan,
Alas! my hairt is gone
*   For ever and aye.*

Through languor of my sweet
So thirlit is my spreit,
My days are most complete
*   Through her absence:*
Christ sen sho knew my smart,
Ingravit in my hairt,
Because I must depairt,
*   From her presence.*

Adieu, my awin sweet thing,
My joy and comforting,
My mirth and solacing
*   Of erdly gloir:*
Fair weel, my lady bricht,
And my remembrance richt;
Fare weel and have gude nicht:
*   I say no more.*

Alexander Scott

George Tsargas manages to take Swinburne's sentiments one step further. Tsargas adds a note of good-riddance to the goodbye that is both refreshing and welcomed:

(now that it's over)
i don't wish to imply
that there aren't good
things about you
or that you're not
an extraordinary person
but i'd rather
let other people
enjoy the surprise

George Tsargas

More often than not, readers come to goodbye poetry with a detached, impersonal outlook, not always realizing that each of the poems could express a greater range of feeling if only they were put in the context of the poet's life. The English poet, George Crabbe, had proposed marriage to Charlotte Ridout. She accepted. But when away from her Crabbe had doubts and as his biographer, Rene Huchon, says, "he sacrificed his passion to his misgivings and preserved his freedom." Crabbe composed the following poem on saying goodbye to Charlotte:

Yes! I must go — it is a part
That cruel Fortune has assign'd me, —
Must go, and leave, with aching heart,
What most that heart adores behind me.

Still I shall see thee on the sand
Till o'er the space the water rises,
Still shall in thought behind thee stand,
And watch the look affection prizes.

But ah! what youth attends thy side
With eyes that speak his soul's devotion —
To thee as constant as the tide
That gives the restless wave its motion?

Still in thy train must he appear,
For every gazing, smiling, talking?
Ah! would that he were sighing here,
And I were there beside thee walking!

Wilt thou to him that arm resign,
Who is to that dear heart a stranger,
And with those matchless looks of thine
The peace of this poor youth endanger!

Away this fear that fancy makes
When night and death's dull image hide thee:
In sleep, to thee my mind awakes;
Awake, it sleeps to all beside thee.

Who could in absence bear the pain
Of all this fierce and jealous feeling,
But for the hope to meet again
And see those smiles all sorrow healing?

Then shall we meet, and, heart to heart,
Lament that fate such friends should sever,
And I shall say — 'We must not part';
And thou wilt answer — 'Never, never!'

George Crabbe

The story of William Cowper's romance with his cousin, Theodora Jane, is not a happy one. Theodora's father, Ashley Cowper, objected to the match ostensibly because the parties were too nearly related in blood, but more likely because he feared Cowper's hereditary tendency to insanity. Cowper composed this touching farewell to Theodora Jane:

Bid adieu, my sad heart, bid adieu to thy peace!
Thy pleasure is past, and thy sorrows increase;
See the shadows of evening how far they extend,
And a long night is coming that never may end;
For the sun is now set that enliven'd the scene,
And an age must be past e'er it rises again.

Already deprived of its splendour and heat,
I feel thee more slowly, more heavily beat;
Perhaps over strain'd with the quick pulse of pleasure,
Thou art glad of this respite to beat at thy leisure;
But the sigh of distress shall now weary thee more,
Than the flutter and tumult of passion before.

The heart of a lover is never at rest,
With joy overwhelm'd or with sorrow oppress'd;
When Delia is near, all is ecstacy then,
And I even forget I must lose her again.
When absent, as wretched, as happy before,
Despairing I cry, I shall see her no more!

William Cowper

The goodbye poem, as we have seen, takes on many forms. All are equally expressive of the plight of the rejected lover, though some manage to convey emotion in a rather more dignified fashion than others. Elinor Wylie's *Felo De Se* and Robert Browning's *The Lost Mistress* are superlative, while Harold Munro's *The Terrible Door* and Edward Thomas' *Like a Touch of Rain* are sad in their tone of self-pity. One last type of goodbye poem remains to be heard from, and that is the goodbye to love itself. Tired of being pin cushions to Cupid's little darts, many men and women have shrugged their shoulders and turned their backs on love. Sir Thomas Wyatt's *A Renouncing of Love* and Samuel Taylor Coleridge's *Farewell to*

Love have obvious similarities, and both bear the mark of the experienced and world-wise cynic:

A RENOUNCING OF LOVE

Farewell, Love, and all thy laws for ever:
They baited hooks shall tangle me no more;
Senec and Plato call me from thy lore,
To perfect wealth my wit for to endeavour.
In blind error when I did persever,
Thy sharp repulse, that pricketh ay so sore,
Hath taught me to set in trifles no store,
And scape forth, since liberty is lever.
Therefore, farewell: go trouble younger hearts,
And in me claim no more authority;
With idle youth go use thy property,
And thereon spend thy many brittle darts;
For hitherto though I have lost all my time,
Me lusteth no longer rotten boughs to climb.

Sir Thomas Wyatt

FAREWELL TO LOVE

Farewell, sweet Love! yet blame you not my truth;
  More fondly ne'er did mother eye her child
Than I your form: yours were my hopes of youth,
  And as you shaped my thoughts, I sighed or smiled.
While most were wooing wealth, or gaily swerving
  To pleasure's secret haunt, and some apart
Stood strong in pride, self-conscious of deserving,
  To you I gave my whole weak wishing heart;
And when I met the maid that realised
  Your fair creations, and had won her kindness,
Say but for her if aught on earth I prized!
  Your dreams alone I dreamt, and caught your blindness.
O grief — but farewell, Love! I will go play me
  With thoughts that please me less, and less betray me.

Samuel Taylor Coleridge

John Fletcher was the equal of Wyatt and Coleridge in his cynicism and his censure of love. In *The Sad Song* he says goodbye to a love that is forever telling "lie after lie":

THE SAD SONG

Away delights, go seek some other dwelling,
  For I must die:
Farewell, false Love, thy tongue is ever telling
  Lie after lie.
For ever let me rest now from they smarts,
  Alas, for pity go,
  And fire their hearts
That have been hard to thee, mine was no so.

Never again deluding love shall know me,
  For I will die;
And all those griefs that think to over-grow me,
  Shall be as I;
For ever will I sleep, while poor maids cry,
  Alas, for pity stay,
    And let us die
With thee, men cannot mock us in the clay.

John Fletcher

Christina Rossetti's *An End* is much less angry and more accepting of the death of love. Her poem is a lament, yet recognizes that love, once dead, must be buried and, though fondly, only infrequently recalled:

AN END

Love, strong as Death, is dead.
Come, let us make his bed
Among the dying flowers:
A green turf at his head;
And a stone at his feet,
Whereon we may sit
In the quiet evening hours.

He was born in the spring,
And died before the harvesting:
On the last warm summer day
He left us; he would not stay
For autumn twilight cold and grey.
Sit we by his grave, and sing
He is gone away.

To few chords and sad and low
Sing we so:
Be our eyes fixed on the grass
Shadow-veiled as the years pass,
While we think of all that was
In the long ago.

Christina Rossetti

Chapter 2

"And please do not write back. There can be nothing more to say."

Dora Carrington

Love letters are anything but impersonal and, as Etienne Ray observed, "the only love letters which have any use are letters of good-bye." Next to the vibrant emotions of farewell letters all other epistles pale by comparison. Each letter speaks volumes, paying service to the frustration, loneliness, pain and sorrow of a neglected or rejected lover. But perhaps no letters of goodbye are as pointedly expressive as those that are written from the scaffold. These gallows letters are a part of our past; they tell a story of love and life sacrificed on the altars of political and religious belief; they are eloquent and simple; and they humanize history.

Chidiock Tichborne was arrested for his part in the Babington plot, which was designed to overthrow Elizabeth I and put Mary Stuart on the throne. He was executed the day after he wrote this letter to his wife:

[1586]

To ye most lovinge wife alive, I commend me unto her and desire God to blesse her with all happiness, pray for her dead husband and be of good comfort, for I hope in Jesus Christ this morning, to see the face of my Maker and redeemer in the most joyfull throan of his glorious kingdome....

Deere wife forgive me, that hath by these meanes impoverished her fortunes; patience and pardon good wife I crave, make of these our necesseties a virtue, and lay no further burthen on my necke than hath alreadie borne, there be certaine debts that I owe; because I knowe not the order of the Lawe. Piteouse it hath taken from me all, forfeited by my course of offense to Her Majesty....

Now Sweet Cheeke, what is left now to bestowe on thee, a Small joynture, a Small recompense for thy deserving, these legacies followinge to be thine owne. God of his infinite goodnes give thee grace alwaies to remaine his true and faithfull Servant who, that through the merites of his bitter and blessed passion, thou maiest become ... of his kingdom with the blessed women in heaven....

May the Holy Ghost comfort thee with all necessaries for the wealth of thy soul in the World to come, where untill it shall please almighty god I meet thee, farewell lovinge Wife, ffarewell the dearest to me on all ye Earthe, ffarewell, by the hand from the hearte of the most faithfull lovinge husbande

Chideock Ticheburn

Sir Walter Raleigh's farewell letter to his wife, Lady Elizabeth Raleigh, was a bit premature. He lived in confinement in the Tower of London until 1616, when he was released to search for gold. The failure of his expedition led to his execution in 1618:

[1603]

You shall now receive (my deare wife) my last words in these my last lines. My love I send you that you may keep it when I am dead, and my councell that you may remember it when I am no more. I would not by my will present you with sorrowes (dear Besse) let them go to the grave with me and be buried in the dust. And seeing that it is not Gods will that I should see you any more in this life, beare it patiently, and with a heart like thy selfe.

First, I send you all the thankes which my heart can conceive, or my words can reherse for your many travailes, and care taken for me, which though they have not taken effect as you wished, yet my debt to you is not the lesse: but pay it I never shall in this world. . . .

But take heed of the pretences of men, and their affections, for they last not but in honest and worthy men, and no greater misery can befall you in this life, than to become a prey, and afterwards to be despised. I speake not this (God knowes) to dissuade you from marriage, for it will be best for you, both in respect of the world and of God. As for me, I am no more yours, nor you mine, death hath cut us asunder: and God hath divided me from the world, and you from me. . . .

I cannot write much, God he knows how hardly I steale this time while others sleep, and it is also time that I should separate my thoughts from the world. Begg my dead body which living was denied thee; and either lay it at Sherburne (and if the land continue) or in Exeter-Church, by my Father and Mother; I can say no more, time and death call me away.

The everlasting God, powerfull, infinite, and omnipotent God, That Almighty God, who is goodness it selfe, the true life and true light keep thee and thine: have mercy on me, and teach me to forgive my persecutors and false accusers, and send us to meet in his glorious Kingdome. My deare wife farewell. Blesse my poore boy. Pray for me, and let my good God hold you both in his armes.

Written with the dying hand of sometimes thy Husband, but now alasse overthrowne.

Yours that was, but now not my own.
Walter Rawleigh

John Penruddock was a Royalist who led an armed force on the side of the exiled King Charles II. He was captured by Cromwell's New Model Army and beheaded. His last letter to his wife is among the most beautiful and touching letters in the English language:

4th May 1655

Dearest Best of Creatures!

I had taken leave of the world when I receieved yours; it did at once recall my fondness to life, and enable me to resign it. As I am sure I shall leave none behind me like you, which weakens my resolution to part from you, so when I reflect I am going to a place where there are none but such as you, I recover my courage. But fondness breaks in upon me; and as I would not have my tears flow to-morrow, when your husband and the father of our dear babes is a public spectacle, do not think meanly of me, that I give way to grief now in private, when I see my sand run so fast, and within a few hours I am to leave you helpless and exposed to the merciless and insolent that have wrongfully put me to a shameful death, and will object the shame to my poor children. I thank you for all your goodness to me, and will endeavour so to die as to do nothing unworthy that virtue in which we have mutually supported each other, and for which I desire you not to repine that I am first to be rewarded, since you ever preferred me to yourself in all other things. Afford me, with cheerfulness, the precedence of this. I desire your prayers in the article of death; for my own will then be offered for you and yours.

In spite of the efforts of Madame Desmoulins to save his life, Camille Desmoulins was executed for his part in the French Revolution the day after writing the following letter. Madame Desmoulins was guillotined two weeks later.

On the 2nd Germinal, the II Decade,
at 5 o'clock in the morning 1 April, 1794
Beneficent slumber has helped me to obliterate my sufferings. When one sleeps, one has not the feeling of being in prison, one is free. Heaven had mercy on me. Only a moment ago, I saw you in my dream, I embraced you one after another. . . . Our little one had lost an eye, and I saw it in a bandage. And in my distress at this, I woke up. I found myself in my dungeon. Day was dawning. I saw you no more, my Lolotte, and could not hear you, for you and your mother, you had spoken to me, and Horace, without feeling his pain, had said, 'Papa, papa.' Oh, these cruel ones, who deprive me of the joy to hear these words, to see you and to make you happy. For that was my only ambiiton and my only conspiracy. . . .

I was born in order to make you happy, in order to create for us both, with your mother and my father and some intimate friends, a Tahiti. I dreamed the dreams of the Abbé Saint-Pierre. I dreamed of a republic, the idol of all men; I could not believe that men are so unjust and so cruel. . . .

Pardon me, my dear one, my true life, that I lost when we were separated, for occupying myself with memory. I had far better busy myself in making you forget. My Lucile, my dear Louploup, my darling, I implore you, do not call upon me; your cries will rend my heart even at the bottom of my grave. Care for your little one; live for my Horace; speak to him of me. Tell him hereafter what he cannot now understand, that I should have loved him well. Notwithstanding my punishment, I believe there is a God. My blood will wash out my faults, my human weakness, and for the good I have done, for my virtues, my love of Liberty, God will reward me. I shall see you again one day. O Lucile!... Feeling as I do, is death so great a misfortune, since it delivers me from the sight of so many enemies?

Good-bye, Louploup, my life, my soul, my heaven on earth! I leave you to good friends — all the sensible and virtuous men who remain. Good-bye — Lucile, my Lucile, my dear Lucile. . . . The shores of life recede from me. I see you still, Lucile, my beloved. My bound hands embrace you, and my head as it falls rests its dying eyes upon you.

Much has been written on the death of Sir Thomas More, who was executed in 1535 for refusing to take the oath repudiating papal supremacy. The day before he died he wrote this goodbye letter to his daughter, Margaret Roper:

[1535]

. . . I cumber you, good Margaret, much, but I would be sorry if it should be any longer than tomorrow. For it is Saint Thomas' even and the Utas of Saint Peter; and therefore tomorrow long I to go to God: it were a day very meet and convenient for me. I never liked your manner toward me better than when you kissed me last: for I love when daughterly love and dear charity hath no leisure to look to worldly courtesy. Farewell, my dear child, and pray for me, and I shall for you and all your friends, that we may merrily meet in Heaven. I thank you for your great cost. . . .

For all their tragedy and violence, gallows goodbyes have a serenity unmatched in farewell letters penned by other lovers. The following epistles, written by husbands who have departed from their wives and by wives who must leave their husbands, express a sadness and emptiness that is extremely moving.

Catherine of Aragon, Henry VIII's first wife, did not fare well at the hands of her beloved husband. Yet throughout the humiliations that he heaped upon her — the divorce, exile from court, separation from her daughter Mary — she remained devoted to him. She wrote him this letter shortly before her death:

[*1535*]

My Lord and Dear Husband,

I commend me unto you. The hour of my death draweth fast on, and my case being such, the tender love I owe you forceth me, with a few words, to put you in remembrance of the health and safeguard of your soul, which you ought to prefer before all worldly matters, and before the care and tendering of your own body, for the which you have cast me into many miseries and yourself into many cares.

For my part I do pardon you all, yea, I do wish and devoutly pray God that He will also pardon you.

For the rest I commend unto you Mary, our daughter, beseeching you to be a good father unto her, as I heretofore desired. I entreat you also, on behalf of my maids, to give them marriage-portions, which is not much, they being but three. For all my other servants, I solicit a year's pay more than their due, lest they should be unprovided for.

Lastly, do I vow, that mine eyes desire you above all things.

Laurence Sterne had a rather indiscreet, if somewhat economical habit of copying from his original love letters to his wife, Elizabeth Lumley, to send to later lovers. The following letter was written to Elizabeth after her departure for Staffordshire in 1740. Their separation, although only temporary, transported Sterne to depths of despair that could not have been equaled had the goodbye been permanent:

[*1740*]

You bid me tell you, my dear L., how I bore your departure for S——, and whether the valley where D'Estella stands, retains still its looks — or, if I think the roses or jessamines smell as sweet as when you left it. Alas! every thing has now lost its relish and look! The hour you left D'Estella, I took to my bed. I was worn out by fevers of all kinds, but most by that fever of the heart which thou knowest well I have been wasting these two years — and shall continue wasting till you quit S——. . . .

I ∴ . . returned home to your lodgings (which I have hired till your return) to resign myself to misery. Fanny had prepared me a supper — she is all attention to me — but I sat over it with tears; a bitter sauce, my L., but I could eat it with no other — for the moment she began to spread my little table, my heart fainted within me. One solitary plate, one knife, one fork, one glass! I gave a thousand pensive penetrating looks at the chair thou hadst so often graced, in those quiet and sentimental repasts — then laid down my knife and fork, and took out my handkerchief, and clapped it across my face, and wept like a child. I do so this very moment, my L.; for, as I take up my pen, my poor pulse quickens, my pale face glows, and tears are trickling down upon the paper as I trace the word L——. O thou, blessed in thyself, and in thy virtues — blessed to all that know thee — to me most so, because more do I know of thee than all thy sex. This is the philtre, my L., by which thou hast charmed me, and by which thou wilt hold me thine, whilst virtue and faith hold this world together. This, my friend, is the plain and simple magic, by which I told Miss—— I have won a place in that heart of thine, on which I depend so satisfied, that time, or distance, or change of every thing which might alarm the hearts of little men, create no uneasy suspence in mine. Wast thou to stay in S—— these seven years, thy friend, though he would grieve, scorns to doubt or to be doubted — 'tis the only exception where security is not the parent of danger. I told you poor Fanny was all attention to me since your departure — contrives every day bringing in the name of L. She told me last night (upon giving me some hartshorn) she had observed my illness began the very day of your departure for S——; that I had never held up my head; had seldom, or scarce ever smiled; had fled from all society — that she verily believed I was broken-hearted, for she had never entered the room, or passed by the door, but she heard me sigh heavily — that I neither ate, or slept, or took pleasure in any thing as before. Judge then, my L., can the valley look so well — or the roses and jessamines smell so sweet as heretofore? Ah Me! — But adieu — the vesper bell calls me from thee to my God!

L. Sterne

The great English comic writer, Thomas Hood, dearly loved his wife and her going plainly caused him a great deal of anguish:

[*no date*]

My own dearest and best, — We parted manfully and womanfully as we ought. I drank only half a bottle of the Rhine wine, and only the half of that, ere I fell asleep on the sofa, which lasted two hours. It was the reaction, for your going tired me more than I cared to show. Then I drank the other half, and as that did not do, I went and retraced our walk in the park, and sat down in the same seat, and felt happier and better. Have you not a romantic old husband?

Hood's fondness for taking comfort in familiar haunts is echoed by Victoria Sackville-West, who wrote to her husband, Harold Nicolson, almost daily whenever they were separated. Her letter bears witness that their numerous partings have not dulled the sense of loss that she feels with each new farewell:

25th June, 1929
Long Barn

What is so torturing when I leave you at these London stations and drive off, is the knowledge that you are still there — that, for half an hour or three-quarters of an hour, I could still return and find you; come up behind you, take you by the elbow, and say 'Hadji'.

I came straight home, feeling horribly desolate and sad, driving down that familiar and dreary road. I remembered Rasht and our parting there; our parting at Victoria when you left for Persia; till our life seemed made up of partings, and I wondered how long it would continue.

Then I came round the corner on to the view — our view — and I thought how you loved it, and how simple you were, really, apart from your activity; and how I loved you for being both simple and active in one and the same person.

Then I came home, and it was no consolation at all. You see, when I am unhappy for other reasons, the cottage is a real solace to me; but when it is on account of you that I am unhappy (because you have gone away), it is an additional pang — it is the same place, but a sort of mockery and emptiness hangs about it — I almost wish that just once you could lose me and then come straight back to the cottage and find it still full of me but emtpy of me, then you would know what I go through after you have gone away.

Anyhow, you will say, it is worse for you who go back to a horrible and alien city, whereas I stay in the place we both love so much; but really, Hadji, it is no consolation to come back to a place full of coffee-cups — there was a cardboard-box lid, full of your rose-petals, still on the terrace.

You are dearer to me than anybody ever has been or ever could be. If you died suddenly, I should kill myself as soon as I had made provision for the boys. I really mean this. I could not live if I lost you. I do not think one could conceive of a love more exclusive, more tender, or more pure than I have for you. I think it is immortal, a thing which happens seldom.

Darling, there are not many people who would write such a letter after sixteen years of marriage, yet who would be saying therein only one-fiftieth of what they were feeling as they wrote it. I sometimes try to tell you the truth, and then I find that I have no words at my command which could possibly convey it to you.

Such comforts as those enjoyed by Hood and Sackville-West in helping to overcome the pain of separation were denied Lady Shigenari. Feeling that she would never again see her husband, Lord Kimura Shigenari, she wrote him this impassioned goodbye letter and then took her own life. Not long after, her husband was killed at war:

[Sixteenth century]
I know that when two wayfarers 'take shelter under the same tree and slake their thirst in the same river' it has all been determined by their karma from a previous life. For the past few years you and I have shared the same pillow as a man and wife who had intended to live and grow old together, and I have become as attached to you as your own shadow. This is what I believed, and I think this is what you have also thought about us.

But now I have learnt about the final enterprise on which you have decided and, though I cannot be with you to share the grand moment, I rejoice in the knowledge of it. It is said that (on the eve of his final battle) the Chinese general, Hsiang Yü, valiant warrior though he was, grieved deeply about leaving Lady Yü, and that (in our own country) Kiso Yoshinaka lamented his parting from Lady Matsudono. I have now abandoned all hope about our future together in this world, and (mindful of their example) I have re-solved to take the ultimate step while you are still alive. I shall be waiting for you at the end of what they call the road to death.

I pray that you may never, never forget the great bounty, deep as the ocean, high as the mountains, that has been bestowed upon us for so many years by our lord, Prince Hideyori.

To Lord Shigenari, Governor of Nagato
From His Wife

The torment of unrequited love has led to many farewell letters in which the unassailable hopelessness of the situation is illuminated by pleas, regrets and the chance to take one last shot at the stony-hearted loved one.

Prior to her marriage to the philosopher William Godwin, Mary Wollstonecraft had lived with an American, Captain Gilbert Imlay, whom she had met in Paris. After the birth of their child, Imlay tired of Mary and she returned to London where she twice tried to kill herself. This goodbye letter to Imlay reflects what she called her "living death":

London, November 1795
Sunday morning
I have only to lament, that, when the bitterness of death was past, I was inhumanly brought back to life and misery. But a fixed deter-mination is not to be baffled by disappointment; nor will I allow that to be a frantic attempt which was one of the calmest acts of reason. In this respect, I am only accountable to myself. Did I care for what is termed reputation, it is by other circumstances that I should be dishonoured.

You say, 'that you know not how to extricate ourselves out of the wretchedness into which we have been plunged.' You are extricated long since. But I forbear to comment. If I am condemned to live longer, it is a living death.

It appears to me that you lay much more stress on delicacy than on principle; for I am unable to discover what sentiment of delicacy would have been violated by your visitng a wretched friend, if indeed you have any friendship for me. But since your new attachment is the only sacred thing in your eyes, I am silent — Be happy! My complaints shall never more damp your enjoyment; perhaps I am mistaken in supposing that even my death could, for more than a moment. This is what you call magnanimity. It is happy for yourself, that you possess this quality in the highest desgree.

Your continually asserting that you will do all in your power to contribute to my comfort, when you only allude to pecuniary assistance, appears to me a flagrant breach of delicacy. I want not such vulgar comfort, nor will I accept it. I never wanted but your heart — That gone, you have nothing more to give. Had I only poverty to fear, I should not shrink from life. Forgive me then, if I say, that I shall consider any direct or indirect attempt to supply my necessities, as an insult which I have not merited, and as rather done out of tenderness for your own reputation, than for me. Do not mistake me; I do not think that you value money, therefore I will not accept what you do not care for, though I do much less, because certain privations are not painful to me. When I am dead, respect for yourself will make you take care of the child.

I write with difficulty — probably I shall never write to you again. Adieu!

God bless you!

Benjamin Disraeli was more fortunate. His long and eloquent farewell letter to Mary Anne Wyndham Lewis touched her heart and, later that same year, they were married. Miss Wyndham Lewis possessed considerable financial resources, and Disraeli was quite concerned that he not be thought a fortune hunter. Although he insists that his letter is like a scaffold goodbye, written "as if it were the night before my execution," his urgency betrays the calmness and serenity that we have seen in the letters of Tichborne and Raleigh:

[Park Street. Thursday night, 7 February, 1839]
I wd have endeavoured to have spoken to you of that which it was necessary you shd know, & I wished to have spoken with the calmness which was natural to one humiliated & distressed. I succeeded so far as to be considered a 'selfish bully' & to be desired to quit your house for ever. I have recourse therefore to this miserable method of communicating with you; none can be more imperfect but I write as if it were the night before my execution. . . .

Upon your general conduct to me I make no comment. It is now useless. I will not upbraid you. I will only blame myself. All warned me: public and private — all were eager to save me from the perdition into which I have fallen. Coxcomb to suppose that you wd conduct yourself to me in a manner different to that in which you have behaved to fifty others!

And yet I thought I had touched your heart! Wretched Idiot!

As a woman of the world you must have foreseen this. And for the gratification of your vanity, for the amusement of ten months, for the diversion of your seclusion, could you find the heart to do this? Was there no ignoble prey at hand that you must degrade a bird of heaven? Why not have let your Captain Neil have been the minion of your gamesome hours with humiliating & debasing me. Nature never intended me for a toy & dupe. But you have struck deep. You have done that which my enemies have yet failed to do: you have broken my spirit. From the highest to the humblest scene of my life, from the brilliant world of fame to my own domestic hearth, you have poisoned all. I have no place of refuge: home is odious, the world oppressive.

Triumph — I seek not to conceal my state. It is not sorrow, it is not wretchedness; it is anguish, it is the endurance of that pang which is the passing characteristic of agony. All that can prostrate a man has fallen on my victim head. My heart outraged, my pride wounded, my honor nearly tainted. I know well that ere a few days can pass I shall be the scoff & jest of that world, to gain whose admiration has been the effort of my life. I have only one source of solace — the consciousness of self-respect. Will that uphold me? A terrible problem that must quickly be solved.

Farewell. I will not affect to wish you happiness for it is not in your nature to obtain it. For a few years you may flutter in some frivolous circle. But the time will come when you will sigh for any heart that could be fond and despair of one that can be faithful. Then will be the penal hour of retribution; then you will recall to your memory the passionate heart that you have forfeited, and the genius you have betrayed.

D

Disraeli lived a happy and fulfilled life with Mary Anne. Fate was not so kind to Dora Carrington, whose attachment for Lytton Strachey caused her considerable grief. She went to live with Strachey in 1917 but later left him to marry Ralph Partridge. Strachey died of cancer in 1932; Carrington shot herself a month later. In the following letter addressed to Strachey, Miss Carrington pours out her anguish at being separated from him:

Saturday morning, 12 o'ck [14 May, 1921]
The Mill House, Tidmarsh
My dearest Lytton, There is a great deal to say and I feel very incompetent to write it today. Last night I composed a great many

letters to you, almost till three in the morning. I then wrote an imaginary letter and bared my very soul to you. This morning I don't feel so intimate. You mayn't value my pent up feelings and a tearful letter. I rather object to them not being properly received and left about. . . .

Why am I raking all this up now? Only to tell you that all these years I have known all along that my life with you was limited. I could never hope for it to become permanent. After all Lytton, you are the only person who I have ever had an all absorbing passion for. I shall never have another. I couldn't now. I had one of the most self abasing loves that a person can have. You could throw me into transports of happiness and dash me into deluges of tears and despair, all by a few words. But these aren't reproaches. For after all it's getting on for 6 years since I first met you at Asheham; and that's a long time to be happy. . . .

Still it's too much of a strain to be quite alone here waiting to see you or craning my nose and eyes out of the top window at 41 Gordon Square to see if you are coming down the street, when I know we'll be better friends, if you aren't haunted by the idea that I am sitting depressed in some corner of the world waiting for your footstep. . . .

I cried to think of a savage cynical fate which made it impossible for my love ever to be used by you. You never knew, or never will know the very big and devastating love I had for you. How I adored every hair, every curl on your beard. How I devoured you whilst you read to me at night. How I loved the smell of your face in your sponge. Then the ivory skin on your hands, your voice, and your hat when I saw it coming along the top of the garden wall from my window. Say you will remember it, that it wasn't all lost and that you'll forgive me for this out burst, and always be my friend. Just thinking of you now makes me cry so I can't see this paper, and yet so happy that the next moment I am calm. . . .

Charles Lamb, however, seemed to be able to take rejection with his usual good humor. He had written to the actress Miss Kelly on July 20, 1819, proposing marriage but an "early and deeply rooted attachment" led her to reject him. Lamb replied:

July 20th, 1819

Dear Miss Kelly,
    Your injunctions shall be obeyed to a tittle. I feel myself in a lackadaisacal no-how-ish kind of a humour. I believe it is the rain, or something. I had thought to have written seriously, but I fancy I succeed best in epistles of mere fun; puns and that nonsense. You

*will be good friends with us, will you not? let what has past 'break no
bones' between us. You will not refuse us them next time we send for
them?*

Yours very truly,
C. L.

Do you observe the delicacy of not signing my full name?
N.B. Do not paste that last letter of mine into your Book.

The writer William Congreve was very much a man-about-town. One of his
favorite ladies, the singer Arabella Hunt, took a strong dislike to his
constant philandering and bid him a not very courteous farewell. In reply,
Congreve wrote the following apologetic and suppliant goodbye:

[no date]

*Dear Madam — May I presume to beg pardon for the fault I com-
mitted. So foolish a fault that it was below not only a man of sense
but a man; and of which nothing could ever have made me guilty
but the fury of a passion with which none but your lovely self could
inspire me. May I presume to beg pardon for a fault which I can
never forgive myself? To purchase that pardon what would I not
endure? You shall see me prostrate before you, and use me like a
slave while I kiss the dear feet that trample upon me. But if my crime
be too great for forgiveness, as indeed it is very great, deny me not
one dear parting look, let me see you once before I must never see
you more. . . .*

*Jesus! from whence and whither am I fallen? From the hopes of
blissful extasies to black despair! From the expectation of immortal
transports, which none but your dear self can give me, and which
none but he who loves like me could ever so much as think of, to a
complication of cruel passions and the most dreadful condition of
human life.*

*My fault indeed has been very great, and cries aloud for the
severest vengeance. See it inflicted on me: see me despair and die for
that fault. But let me not die unpardon'd, madam; I die for you, but
die in the most cruel and dreadful manner. The wretch that lies
broken on the wheel alive feels not a quarter of what I endure. Yet
boundless love has been all my crime; unjust, ungrateful, barbar-
ous return for it!*

*Suffer me to take my eternal leave of you; when I have done that
how easy will it be to bid all the rest of the world adieu.*

Fortunately, Congreve's indiscretion did not cause the celebrated Miss
Hunt any untoward despair. But infidelity can lead to the most tragic of all
lover's goodbyes, as this anonymous suicide note illustrates:

[Twentieth century]
No wish to die. One of the best of sports, which they all knew. Not in the wrong, the boys will tell you. This b—— at Palmer's Green has sneaked my wife, one of the best in the world; my wife, the first love in the world.

Dora Carrington seemed to be almost as fond of farewells as Lord Byron. She simply could not love Mark Gertler in the ardent manner he desired, and so she said goodbye:

. . . Only I cannot love you as you want me to. You must know one could not do, what you ask, sexual intercourse, unless one does love a man's body. I have never felt any desire for that in my life: I wrote only four months ago and told you all this, you said you never wanted me to take any notice of you when you wrote again; if it was not that you just asked me to speak frankly and plainly I should not be writing. I do love you, but not in the way you want. Once, you made love to me in your studio, you remember, many years ago now. One thing I can never forget, it made me inside feel ashamed, unclean. Can I help it? I wish to God I could. Do not think I rejoice in being sexless, and am happy over this. It gives me pain also. . . .

Do not be angry with me for having written as I have. And please do not write back. There can be nothing more to say.

Lady Caroline Lamb wrote about Lord Byron, "that beautiful pale face will be my fate." But Byron soon tired of Lady Caroline, and had already departed from her by the time he wrote this last, passionate letter:

[August 1812?]
My dearest Caroline,
If tears which you saw and know I am not apt to shed, — if the agitation in which I parted from you, — agitations which you must have perceived through the whole of this most nervous affair, did not commence until the moment of leaving you approached, — if all I have said and done, and am still but too ready to say and do, have not sufficient proved what my real feelings are, and must ever be towards you, my love, I have no other proof to offer. God knows, I wish you happy, and when I quit you, or rather you, from a sense of duty to your husband and mother, quit me, you shall acknowledge the truth of what I again promise and vow, that no other in word or deed, shall ever hold the place in my affections, which is, and shall be, most sacred to you, till I am nothing. I never knew till that moment the madness of my dearest and most beloved friend; I cannot express myself; this is no time for words, but I shall have a pride, a melancholy pleasure, in suffering what you yourself can

scarcely conceive, for you do not know me. I am about to go out with a heavy heart, because my appearing this evening will stop any absurd story which the event of the day might give rise to. Do you think now I am cold and stern and artful? Will even others think so? Will your mother ever — that mother to whom we must indeed sacrifice much, more, much more on my part than she shall ever know or can imagine? 'Promise not to love you!' ah, Caroline, it is past promising. But I shall attribute all concessions to the proper motive, and never cease to feel all that you have already witnessed, and more than can ever be known but to my own heart, — perhaps to yours. May God protect, forgive, and bless you. Ever, and even more than ever,

Your most attached,
Byron

Jonathan Swift managed to break a number of hearts during his lifetime, not the least of which belonged to Hester Vanhomrigh. Swift's continual toying with her expectations brought on a state of nervous exhaustion which led to her death. The following letter, however, was written to Jane Waring, or 'Varina', one of Swift's early loves. When he left Ireland to renew a position with Sir William Temple at Moor Park, he wrote to her this strange letter of farewell:

April 29, 1696

Madam — Impatience is the most inseparable quality of a lover. . . . That dearest object upon which all my prospect of happiness entirely depends, is in perpetual danger to be removed for ever from my sight. Varina's life is daily wasting, and though one just and honourable action would furnish health to her and unspeakable happiness to us both, yet some power that aspires at human felicity has that influence to hold her continually doting upon her cruelty, and me on the cause of it. This fully convinces me of what we are told, that the miseries of man's life are all beaten out on his own anvil. . . .

Would to Heaven you were but awhile sensible of the thoughts into which my present distractions plunge me; they hale me a thousand ways and I am not able to bear them. It is so, by Heaven! the love of Varina is of more tragical consequence than her cruelty. Would to God you had hated and scorned me from the beginning! It was your pity opened the first way to my misfortune, and now your love is finishing my ruin; and is it so then? In a fortnight I must take eternal farewell of Varina, and (I wonder) will she weep at parting, just a little to justify her poor pretence of some affection for me? and will my friends still continue reproaching me for the want of gallantry and neglecting a close siege? How comes it that they all wish us married together, they knowing my circumstances and yours extremely well, and I am sure love you too much, if it be only for my sake, to wish you anything that might cross your interest or your happiness? . . .

The little disguises and affected contradictions of your sex were all (to say the truth) infinitely beneath persons of your pride and mine; paltry maxims that they are, calculated for the rabble of humanity. O Varina, how imagination leads me beyond myself and all my sorrows! It is sunk, and a thousand graves lie open! No, madam, I will give you no more of my unhappy temper, though I derive it all from you.

Farewell, madam, and may love make you awhile forget your temper to do me justice. Only remember that if you still refuse to be mine you will quickly lose, for ever lose, him that has resolved to die as he has lived all yours.

Jon. Swift

Mary Anne Fitzherbert, 'Margaritta', was in despair over the seeming hopelessness of her relationship with George, Prince of Wales (later George IV). She was a Roman Catholic, and the Act of Settlement stated that if the Prince married a Catholic, he forfeited the succession to the throne. They were, however, secretly married in 1785, but George broke off the marriage in 1794. The following letter, from Margaritta to George, belongs to the period prior to the wedding:

[17——?]

You will compel me to leave B******, I am offended at your behaviour of last night. Why did I seek a walk retired? had we met on the Steine you would have been more guarded; alas! you have not the delicacy I wished! When you talk of love you offer an insult you are insensible of — your friendship confers honour; — but your love — retain it for some worthy fair, born to the high honour of becoming your wife, and repine not that fate has placed my lot — in humble life. I am content with my station: content has charms that are not to be expressed. I know I am wrong in continuing this correspondence; — it must — it ought to cease: write therefore no more to

Margaritta

Events were not so kind to the famous twelfth century lovers, Heloise and Abelard. After their marriage her uncle had Abelard brutally castrated. Heloise retired to a convent, and Abelard roamed from one monastery to another. Their continued correspondence, here displayed in a letter from Heloise to Abelard, helped to soothe their unhappiness.

. . . But if I lose you, what is left for me to hope for? What reason for continuing on life's pilgrimage, for which I have no support but you, and none in you save the knowledge that you are alive, now that I am forbidden all other pleasures in you and denied even the joy of your presence which from time to time could restore me to myself? O God — if I dare say it — cruel to me in everything! O merciless mercy! O Fortune who is only ill-fortune, who has already spent on me so many of the shafts she uses in her battle against mankind that she had none left with which to vent her anger on others. She has emptied a full quiver on me, so that henceforth no one else need fear her onslaughts, and if she still had a single arrow she could find no place in me to take a wound. Her only dread is that through my many wounds death may end my sufferings; and though she does not cease to destroy me, she still fears the destruction which she hurries on.

Of all wretched women I am the most wretched, and amongst the unhappy I am unhappiest. The higher I was exalted when you preferred me to all other women, the greater my suffering over my own fall and yours, when I was flung down; for the higher the ascent, the heavier the fall. Has Fortune ever set any great or noble woman above me or made her my equal, only to be similarly cast down and crushed with grief? What glory she gave me in you, what ruin she brought upon me through you! Violent in either extreme, she showed no moderation in good or evil. To make me the saddest of all women she first made me blessed above all, so that when I thought how much I had lost, my consuming grief would match my crushing loss, and my sorrow for what was taken from me would be the greater for the fuller joy of possession which had gone before; and so that the happiness of supreme ecstasy would end in the supreme bitterness of sorrow.

Chapter 3

"Frankly, my dear, I don't give a damn."

Rhett Butler

Art imitates life; whether this is an accident of convenience or necessity will depend largely upon how you look at either. The lovers' goodbyes we have seen expressed in poetry are intensely economical. They contain no gratuitous wailing or bemoaning, and are always precisely to the point. They distill the essence of saying goodbye and frame it in language and meter, universalizing the sentiments contained in every farewell. Goodbye letters tend to be just the opposite. They are prone to ramble, to be ingratiating and to be private and personal.

Between these two extremes fall the goodbye scenes from fiction, drama and film. Each of these forms offers breadth and room in which to lead up to the goodbye, creating rising emotion and slowly mounting tension. For this reason it would prove unwise to include some famous farewells which, out of context, have very little impact. Those that we have chosen to include are either familiar enough that the context is well known, or self contained to the point that they are capable of standing more or less on their own. We begin with some goodbye letters from fiction.

The letter of the Fair Maid of Astolat in Sir Thomas Mallory's *Le Morte d'Arthur* expresses one young woman's way of saying goodbye in the face of an unfortunate love. She had fallen in love with Sir Lancelot and, realizing the hopelessness of her love, decided to end her life. With a letter clasped in her hand, she was placed in a barge which carried her down the Thames river. There she was seen by King Arthur and Queen Guenevere, who took from her this letter:

> *Most noble knight, Sir Launcelot, now hath death made us two at debate for your love. I was your lover, that men called the fair maiden of Astolat; therefore unto all ladies I make my moan, yet pray for my soul and bury me at least, and offer ye my masspenny: this is my last request. And a clene maiden I died, I take God to witness: pray for my soul, Sir Launcelot, as thou art peerless.*

Hopefully, such unrequited love no longer demands such sacrifices. In Jean Rhys' novel *Voyage in the Dark*, Walter's goodbye to Anna is oddly fashioned in a letter written by his friend, Vincent:

My dear Anna,
—— This is a very difficult letter to write because I am afraid I am going to upset you and I hate upsetting people. We've been back for nearly a week but Walter hasn't been at all well and I have persuaded him to let me write to you and explain matters. I'm quite sure you are a nice girl and that you will be understanding about this. Walter is still very fond of you but he doesn't love you like that any more, and after all you must always have known that the thing could not go on for ever and you must remember too that he is nearly twenty years older than you are. I'm sure that you are a nice girl and that you will think it over calmly and see that there is nothing to be tragic or unhappy or anything like that about. You are young and youth as everybody says is the great thing, the greatest gift of all. The greatest gift, everybody says. And so it is. You've got everything in front of you, lots of happiness. Think of that. Love is not everything — especially that sort of love — and the more people, especially girls, put it right out of their heads and do without it the better. That's my opinion. Life is chock-full of other things, by dear girl, friends and just good times and being jolly together and so on and games and books. Do you remember when we talked about books? I was sorry when you told me that you never read because, believe me, a good book like that book I was talking about can make a lot of difference to your point of view. It makes you see what is real and what is just imaginary. My dear Infant, I am writing this in the country, and I can assure you that when you get into a garden and smell the flowers and all that all this rather beastly sort of love simply doesn't matter. However, you will think I'm preaching at you, so I will shut up. These muddles do happen. They have happened to me, as a matter of fact, worse luck. I can't think why. I can't think why one can't be more sensible. However, I have learnt one thing, that it never helps to let things drag on. Walter has asked me to enclose this cheque for £20 for your immediate expenses because he thinks you may be running short of cash. He will always be your friend and he wants to arrange that you should be provided for and not have to worry about money (for a time at any rate). Write and let him know that you understand. If you really care for him at all you will do this, for believe me he is unhappy about you and he has a lot of other worries as well. Or write me — that would be better still because don't you think it would be just as well for both your sakes if you don't see Walter just now? Then there's that job in

the new show. I want to take you along as soon as possible to see my friend. I think I can promise you that something will come of it. I believe that if you will work hard there is no reason why you should not get on. I've always said that and I stick to it.

Yours ever
Vincent Jeffires

PS *Have you kept any of the letters Walter wrote to you? If so you ought to send them back.*

After Vincent's letter, Anna seems to lose all sense of purpose in life. But at least hers was not the fate of the unfortunate Susan Henchard in Thomas Hardy's *The Mayor of Casterbridge*. Michael Henchard had just cruelly auctioned off his wife and infant daughter, and the following goodbye scene occurs as the buyer is about to take them:

(SUSAN): *Now, before you go Michael, listen to me. If you touch that money, I and this girl go with this man. Mind, it is a joke no longer.*

(HENCHARD): *A joke? Of course it is not a joke. I take the money; the sailor takes you. That's plain enough. It has been done elsewhere — and why not here?*

(SUSAN): *Mike, I've lived with thee a couple of years, and had nothing but temper! Now, I'm no more to 'ee; I'll try my luck elsewhere. 'Twill be better for me and Elizabeth-Jane both. So good-bye!*

Years later, when Susan is dying, she sends Michael this final farewell letter:

My Dear Michael,

For the good of all three of us I have kept one thing a secret from you till now. I hope you will understand why; I think you will; though perhaps you may not forgive me. But, dear Michael, I have done it for the best. I shall be in my grave when you read this, and Elizabeth-Jane shall have a home. Don't curse me Mike — think of how I was situated. I can hardly write it, but here it is. Elizabeth-Jane is not your Elizabeth-Jane — the child who was in my arms when you sold me. No; she died three months after that, and this living one is my other husband's. I christened her by the same name we had given to the first, and she filled my ache at the other's loss. Michael, I am dying, and I might have held my tongue; but could not. Tell her husband of this or not, as you judge; and forgive me, if you can, a woman you once deeply wronged, as she forgives you.

Susan Henchard

In an era that is increasingly visual, one can rightly expect that the silver screen has both fostered and given a broader range to the act of saying goodbye. What Michael Drayton did for the seventeenth century lover, Margaret Mitchell has done for us. Drayton's gentle and evocative "Come let us kiss and part" is a yardstick beside which we can place Rhett Butler's blustry but no less evocative line from *Gone with the Wind:*

Frankly, my dear, I don't give a damn.

So much for the coquettish Scarlett O'Hara!

Just as it is difficult to think of Rhett Butler without thinking of Clark Gable, so it is impossible to call up *Casablanca* without seeing Humphrey Bogart. During the famous airport scene in *Casablanca,* Rick instructs Louis Rennault, The Prefect of Police, to make out the transit papers in the names of Mr. and Mrs. Victor Laszlo. The entire scene builds up to one line, a line that equals "Frankly, my dear, I don't give a damn" as one of the greatest goodbye lines of all time. Rick overrides Ilsa's pleas never to leave him; he gives her the inimitable Bogart look and says:

Here's looking at you, *kid.*

And with that, it is all over but the memories.

Like a modern, though somewhat less than commanding Lord Byron, Woody Allen writes many goodbyes into his screenplays. As *Play it Again Sam* opens, Allen humorously satirizes the break-up of a modern American marriage as Nancy tells her overwhelmed husband, Allan, that she wants a divorce. The scene culminates in this exchange, an exchange which has become a hallmark of the Woody Allen hero — an unassuming, incredulous and somewhat eccentric Don Quixote:

NANCY: *Goodbye, Allan. My lawyer will call your lawyer!*
ALLAN: *I don't have a lawyer. Have him call my doctor.*

It was nothing so romantic as a deep commitment to an earlier love that kept Brett and Jake apart in Ernest Hemingway's novel, *The Sun Also Rises.* Jake's undefined but clearly sex-related war wound leaves a gap in their otherwise happy relationship that neither can bridge. Their goodbye is one of the most simplistically moving farewells in modern literature:

> *The driver started up the street. I settled back. Brett moved close to me. We sat close against each other. I put my arm around her and she rested against me comfortably. It was very hot and bright, and the houses looked sharply white. We turned out onto the Gran Via.*
> *"Oh, Jake," Brett said, "we could have had such a damned good time together."*
> *Ahead was a mounted policeman in Khaki directing traffic. He raised his baton. The car slowed pressing Brett against me.*
> *"Yes," I said. "Isn't it pretty to think so?"*

In a similar way, Catherine's inability to bear children, in François Truffaut's film *Jules and Jim,* leads Jim to say goodbye to her. But Catherine was not about to turn Jim over to Gilberte, and she later kills him in an auto wreck:

> *No, we must look things straight in the face, Catherine. We have failed, we have made a mess of everything. You wanted to change me, to mould me to your needs. On my side, I have brought nothing but suffering to those around me, where I wanted to bring them joy. The promise I made to Gilberte that we would grow old together is worthless, because I can put it off indefinitely. It's a forgery. I no longer hope to marry you. I have to tell you, Catherine, I'm going to marry Gilberte. She and I can still have children.*

Like Jim, Jeanne in Bernardo Bertolucci's *Last Tango in Paris* says goodbye to her lover by telling him that she is going to marry someone else. And like Catherine, Paul is unable to accept the end when it comes. He follows Jeanne home, where she administers the *coup de grâce* by shooting him:

PAUL: *Beauty of mine, sit before me. Let me peruse you and remember you always like this.*

JEANNE: *Oh!*

PAUL: *Waiter, champagne! If music be the food of love, play on! What's the matter with you?*

JEANNE: *It's finished.*

PAUL: *What's the matter with you?*

JEANNE: *It's finished.*

PAUL: *What's finished?*

JEANNE: *We're never going to see each other again, never.*

PAUL: *That's ridiculous. That's ridiculous.*

JEANNE: *It's not a joke.*

PAUL: (jokingly) *Oh, you dirty rat!*

JEANNE: *It's finished.*

PAUL: *Look, when something's finished, it begins again, you see?*

JEANNE: *I'm getting married. I'm going away. It's finished.*

Not all goodbyes are executed in such a violent fashion. Charlie's goodbye to Alice in Daniel Keyes' *Flowers for Algernon* is unique in its combination of self-awareness and sadness. Charlie is quickly reverting to his retarded state that was temporarily altered by an experimental operation. Ironically, it is Charlie and not Alice who is able to recognize and deal with the end when it comes:

"I think it's time for you to leave."

Her face turned red. "Not yet, Charlie. It's not time yet. Don't send me away."

"You're making it harder for me. You keep pretending I can do things and understand things that are far beyond me now. You're pushing me. Just like my mother . . ."

"That's not true!"

"Everything you do says it. The way you pick up and clean up after me, the way you leave books around that you think will get me interested in reading again, the way you talk to me about the news to get me thinking. You say it doesn't matter, but everything you do shows how much it matters. Always the schoolteacher. I don't want to go to concerts or museums or foreign films or do anything that's going to make me struggle to think about life or about myself."

"Charlie —"

"Just leave me alone. I'm not myself. I'm falling apart, and I don't want you here."

That made her cry. This afternoon she packed her bags and left. The apartment feels quiet and empty now.

In Henrik Ibsen's play, *A Doll's House,* Nora escapes her doll-house marriage in a manner wholly unlike that created by Nancy when she left Allan in *Play it Again Sam.* Ibsen draws on Nordic sombreness and melancholy where Woody Allen uses humorous satire:

NORA: *That's right. Now it is all over I have put the keys here.*

HELMER: *All over! All over! — Nora, shall you never think of me again?*

NORA: *I know I shall often think of you and the children and this house.*

HELMER: *May I write to you, Nora?*

NORA: *No — Never. You must not do that.*

HELMER: *But at least let me send you —*

NORA: *Nothing — nothing —*

HELMER: *Let me help you if you are in want.*

NORA: *No. I can receive nothing from a stranger.*

HELMER: *Nora — can I never be anything more than a stranger to you?*

NORA: *Ah, Torvald, the most wonderful thing of all would have to happen.*

HELMER: *Tell me what that would be!*

NORA: *Both you and I would have to be so changed that — Oh, Torvald, I don't believe any longer in wonderful things happening.*

HELMER: *But I will believe in it. Tell me. So changed that — ?*

NORA: *That our life together would be a real wedlock. Good-bye.*

HELMER: *Nora! Nora! . . . Empty. She is gone.*

But tragedy plays a large part in the literary goodbye, and perhaps it is nowhere more evident than in the works of Charles Dickens and William Shakespeare. In Dicken's novel, *A Tale of Two Cities,* the little seamstress goes to the guillotine with Sydney Carton. She is aware that Carton is taking Charles Darnay's place, and finds comfort in his brave sacrifice. This goodbye is among the most memorable in literature:

"You comfort me so much! I am so ignorant. Am I to kiss you now? Is the moment come?"

"Yes."

She kisses his lips; he kisses hers; they solemnly bless each other. The spare hand does not tremble as he releases it; nothing worse than a sweet, bright constancy is in the patient face. She goes next before him — is gone; the knitting-women count Twenty-Two.

"I am the Resurrection and the Life, saith the Lord: he that believeth in me, though he were dead, yet shall he live: and whosoever liveth and believeth in me shall never die."

The murmuring of many voices, the upturning of many faces, the pressing on of many footsteps in the outskirts of the crowd, so that it swells forward in a mass, like one great heave of water, all flashes away. Twenty-Three.

Carton exits with these remarkable words:

It is a far, far better thing that I do, than I have ever done; it is a far, far better rest that I go to, than I have ever known.

Next to Byron, Shakespeare is the most likely candidate for the farewelling crown of English literature. While everybody has their own favorite good-bye scenes from Shakespeare, the few included here are among the best known.

Lear's abrupt goodbye to Cordelia underlines the full sense of tragedy that dominates *King Lear:*

LEAR: *Thou hast her, France. Let her be thine for we*
Have no such daughter, nor shall ever see
That face of hers again. Therefore be gone
Without our grace, our love, our benison.

In *Hamlet,* Gertrude, Queen of Denmark, scatters flowers over the grave of Ophelia and leaves her with these famous parting words:

Sweets to the sweet: farewell!
I hop'd thou shouldst have been my Hamlet's wife,
I thought thy bride-bed to have deck'd, sweet maid,
And not have strew'd thy grave.

Yet the most heart-breaking goodbye in all of Shakespeare must belong to Romeo and Juliet. By far the more memorable parting words are Juliet's. Early in the play she takes her leave of Romeo:

Good night, good night! Parting is such sweet sorrow
That I shall say good night till it be morrow.

Later Romeo finds Juliet in the Capulet tomb and, thinking her to be dead, takes his final leave of her:

Ah! dear Juliet,
Why art thou yet so fair? Shall I believe
That unsubstantial Death is amorous,
And that the lean abhorred monster keeps
Thee here in dark to be his paramour?
For fear of that I still will stay with thee,

And never from this palace of dim night
Depart again: here, here will I remain
With worms that are thy chambermaids; O! here
Will I set up my everlasting rest,
And shake the yoke of inauspicious stars
From this world-wearied flesh. Eyes, look your last!
Arms, take your last embrace! and, lips, O you
The doors of breath, seal with a righteous kiss
A dateless bargain to engrossing death!
Come, bitter conduct, come, unsavoury guide!
Thou desperate pilot, now at once run on
The dashing rocks thy sea-sick weary bark!
Here's to my love! [Drinks.] O true apothecary!
Thy drugs are quick. Thus with a kiss I die.

Juliet awakens from her drug-induced sleep and, seeing Romeo dead beside her, speaks her plaintive farewell:

Where is my Romeo? . . .
What's here? a cup, clos'd in my true love's hand?
Poison, I see, hath been his timeless end.
O churl! drunk all and left no friendly drop
To help me after! I will kiss thy lips;
Haply, some poison yet doth hang on them,
To make me die with a restorative. [Kisses him.]
Thy lips are warm!
. . . . .
Yea, noise? then I'll be brief. O happy dagger!
[Snatching Romeo's dagger]
This is thy sheath; [Stabs herself.] there rest
and let me die.

In more recent literature young lovers have parted in somewhat less than tragic circumstances. In Philip Roth's novel, *Goodbye, Columbus,* Neil and Brenda say goodbye to each other after arguing about her contraceptive diaphragm:

"Neil, what are you talking about! You're the one who doesn't understand. You're the one who from the very beginning was accusing me of things? Remember? Isn't it so? Why don't you have your eyes fixed? As if it were my fault that I could have them fixed. *You kept acting as if I was going to run away from you every minute. And now you're doing it again, telling me I planted that thing on purpose.*
"I loved you, Brenda, so I cared."
"I loved you. That's why I got that damn thing in the first place."

And then we heard the tense in which we'd spoken and we settled back into ourselves and silence.

A few minutes later I picked up my bag and put on my coat. I think Brenda was crying too when I went out the door.

However, Bud and Deanie's goodbye in William Inge's play, *Splendor in the Grass*, is as touching as it is final; it represents a fall from innocence that no amount of back-tracking will recover:

DEANIE: *You're happy, Bud?*

  BUD: *I guess so. I never ask myself that question very often though. How about you?*

DEANIE: *...I'm getting married next month.*

  BUD: *Are you, Deanie?*

DEANIE: *Yes. A boy from Cincinnati. I think you might like him.*

  BUD: *Things work out awfully funny sometimes, don't they, Deanie?*

DEANIE: *Yes, they do.*

  BUD: *I hope you'll be awfully happy, Deanie.*

DEANIE: *Like you, Bud... I don't think too much about happiness either.*

  BUD: *What's the point? You gotta take what comes.*

DEANIE: *Yes... well...*

  BUD: *Deanie! I'm... I'm awfully glad to see you again, Deanie.*

DEANIE: *Thanks, Bud! Good-bye.*

  BUD: *Goodbye.*

Part Two

You won't have Dick Nixon to kick around anymore.

Chapter 4

"People only leave by way of the box — ballot or coffin."

U.S. Senator Claiborne Pell

Thank goodness for scandals and elections.

Without them, politicians would never lose, never resign and never pay speech writers for last drafts.

Politicians would never have to bid farewell to their previously adoring public, thus denying themselves one of the most glorious rewards of defeat — the public goodbye. And since politicians are in many ways created by the public they serve, it is only natural that when their days in office are ended, they would not be content simply to kiss the cheeks of their staffs, clean out their files and walk home alone to pen their memoirs.

The public wouldn't stand for it; the news cameras would have far less to cover on election night; and we would all be denied those real and supposed lessons in humility that yesterday's leaders are so fond of granting us.

What sets political goodbyes apart from others is that the motivation behind them is hardly ever love, and even less, sincerity. On those rare occasions when compassion meets the public eye, it is usually so surrounded by other motivations that it disappears in a sea of semantics.

Yet the use of ten words when one will do is not the sole domain of elected politicians: kings, emperors, dictators, absolute monarchs and their panoply of aides, retainers and hangers-on from every time and place have spared their audience the facts, but not for want of words to hide them under:

Three things can ruin a man — money, power and women. I never had any money. I never wanted power, and the only woman in my life is up at the house right now.

Harry Truman

The moment in which the defamatory campaign seemed to have struck the confidence of political forces, my choice could not be anything but this.

Giovanni Leone, President of Italy,
announcing his resignation,
amid growing financial scandals, in 1978.

A great and proud era is ending and a brave new future (is) beginning.

Ian Smith, on the dissolution of
the Rhodesian government, 1979.

In these decisive days in the life of Russia, we have thought it a duty of conscience to facilitate for your people a close union and consolidation of all national forces for the speedy attainment of victory; and, in agreement with the Imperial Duma, we have thought it good to abdicate from the throne of the Russian State, and to lay down the Supreme power ... May the Lord God help Russia!

Tsar Nicholas II of Russia, on his abdication
from the Throne of Russia, 1918.

Please accept my resignation. I don't want to belong to any club that would accept me as a member.

Groucho Marx, in a telegram.

Real politik is not the only place where the graves of goodbyes abound. Theatre and poetry are littered with princes who gave up all for love. Yet

Edward VIII
&
Mrs Simpson

reality so often intervenes in the lives of real princes that when one really *does* give up his throne for a woman, his words of abdication threaten to become immortal. For Edward VIII, marriage to the American divorcée Wallis Warfield Simpson brought a constitutional crisis to England in 1936 that ended with his abdication. His radio broadcast to his subjects marked the first time in British history that a king has given up his throne for love:

> *. . . You must believe me when I tell you that I have found it impossible to carry the heavy burden of responsibility and to discharge my duties as King as I would wish to do, without the help of the woman I love.*
>
> Edward VIII

His official resignation was more regal in tone:

> *Realizing as I do the gravity of this step, I can now only hope that I shall have the understanding of my people in the decision I have taken and the reasons which have led me to take it.*
>
> *I will not enter now into my private feeling, but I would beg that it should be remembered that the burden which constantly rests upon the shoulders of a sovereign is so heavy that it can only be borne in circumstances different from those in which I now find myself. I conceive that I am not overlooking the duty that rests on me to place in the forefront public interest when I declare that I am conscious that I can no longer discharge this heavy task with efficiency or with satisfaction to myself.*
>
> *I have accordingly this morning executed an instrument of abdication in the terms following:*
>
> *I, Edward VIII, of Great Britain, Ireland, and British Dominions beyond the seas, King and Emperor of India, do hereby declare my irrevocable determination to renounce the throne for myself and for my descendants and my desire that should be given to this instrument of abdication immediately.*
>
> *In token whereof I have hereunto set my hand this tenth day of December, 1936, in the presence of the witnesses whose signatures are subscribed. . . .*
>
> Edward VIII

Whether king by title or king by fact, the royal farewell bears an important mark through history:

*Friends, Romans, countrymen, lend me your ears; I come to bury
Caesar, not to praise him.
The evil that men do lives after them;
The good is oft interred with their bones;
So let it be with Caesar.*

Mark Antony's oration on the dead body of
Julius Caesar

*. . . Nay, then, farewell!
I have touched the highest point of all my greatness;
And now, from that full meridian of my glory,
I haste now to my setting; I shall fall
Like a bright exhalation in the evening,
And no man see me more.*

Wolsey, when his duplicity is discovered,
in Shakespeare's *Henry VIII*

*Soldiers of my Old Guard: I bid you farewell.
For 20 years, I have constantly accompanied you on the road to
honour and glory. In these latter times, as in the days of our
prosperity, you have invariably been models of courage and fidelity.
With men such as you our cause could not be lost; but the war
would have been interminable: it would have been Civil War, and
that would have entailed deeper misfortunes on France.*

I have sacrificed all my interests to those of the country.

*I go, but you, my friends, will continue to serve France. Her happiness was my only thought. It will still be the object of my wishes. Do
not regret my fate; if I have consented to survive, it is to serve your
glory. I intend to write the history of the great achievements we have
performed together. Adieu, my friends. Would I could press you all
to my heart.*

Napoleon Bonaparte, in his farewell address
to the Old Guard.

*When I contemplate you, soldiers, and when I consider your past
exploits, a strong hope of victory animates me. Your spirit, your age,
your valour, give me confidence; to say nothing of necessity, which
makes even cowards brave. To prevent the numbers of the enemy
from surrounding us, our confined situation is sufficient. But
should Fortune be unjust to your valour, take care not to lose your
lives unavenged; take care not to be taken and butchered like cattle,
rather than, fighting like men, to leave your enemies a bloody and
mournful victory.*

Catiline, leader of the famous conspiracy
against the Roman Republic in the first
century, B.C.

Mark Antony, the Late Julius Caesar & Assorted Conspirators

But if ever a country deserved the dubious honor of forced and embarrassing resignations, it was — and is — forever England. When sex is the reason for it, politics makes a familiar bedfellow.

On June 5, 1963, the Secretary of State for War, Mr. John Profumo, rose in the House of Commons and spoke for the first time of his involvement with a twenty-three year old call-girl, Christine Keeler.

In a letter to Prime Minister MacMillan, Profumo admitted the following:

> *You will recollect that on March 22, following certain allegations made in Parliament, I made a public statement. At that time, rumour had charged me with assisting in the disappearance of a witness and with being involved with some possible breach of security.*

> *So serious were these charges that I allowed myself to think that my personal association with that witness, which had also been the subject of rumour, was, by comparison, of minor importance only.*

> *In my statement, I said that there had been no impropriety in this association. To my very deep regret, I have had to admit that this was not true, and that I misled you, and my colleagues, and the House. I ask you to understand that I did this to protect, as I thought, my wife and family, who were equally misled, as were my professional advisers.*

> *I have come to realize that, by this deception, I have been guilty of a grave misdemeanour, and despite the fact that there is no truth whatever in the other charges, I cannot remain a member of your administration, nor of the House of Commons.*

> *I cannot tell you of my deep remorse for the embarrassment I have caused to you, to my colleagues in the Government, to my constituents, and to the Party which I have served for the past 25 years.*

Prime Minister Macmillan wasted no time ridding himself of this eloquent miscreant:

> *The contents of your letter of June 4 have been communicated to me, and I have heard them with deep regret. This is a great tragedy for you, your family and your friends.*

> *Nevertheless, I am sure you will understand that in the circumstances I have no alternative but to advise the Queen to accept your resignation.*

For Jeremy Thorpe, leader of Britain's Liberal Party a decade later, the charges were more serious. He resigned in 1976 after being accused of having a homosexual relationship some years earlier with Norman Scott, a former male model. When the scandal began appearing in the press, Thorpe wrote to his party's acting Chief Whip:

> *... Sections of the press have turned a series of accusations into a sustained witch-hunt, and there are no indications that this will not continue. ... I am convinced that a fixed determination to destroy the leader could itself result in the destruction of the Party. I have always felt that the fortunes of the Party are far more important than any individual, and accordingly, I want to advise you that I am herewith resigning the leadership.*
>
> *... You will know from the very beginning that I have strenuously denied the so-called Scott allegations, and categorically repeat those denials today. ... No man can effectively lead a party if the greater part of his time has to be devoted to answering allegations as they arise and countering continuing plots and intrigues.*

The reply he received was considerably more cheerful than the one which greeted Profumo. But the optimism was premature:

> *Your decision will be received by your colleagues with great sadness. ... Your personal qualities of leadership, charisma and sheer perseverance, and your triumphs over adveristy, are held in high regard by all your colleagues and admired by the public at large. ... I am glad that you are remaining with us as a parliamentary colleague. You will be greatly sustained in the months ahead by your constituents as well as your family, and we all look forward to the time when, freed of your present troubles, you return to a key role in the public life of our country.*

Life went from worse to worse for Thorpe after his resignation. He was accused, along with two others, of conspiring to murder Norman Scott. He ran for office again in the 1979 election, losing miserably against an unknown Conservative. But things began to look brighter when, in June of the same year, he was acquitted of all charges in the Scott case.

Perhaps it is the long winter nights, but Canada has more than its share of halting apologies and halted careers. For Pierre Sevigny, an associate Defence Minister in the early 1960's, the end came when it was revealed that he had had relations with a call-girl named Gerda Munsinger, who was thought to be a Russian agent. Now a Montreal businessman, Sevigny has been exiled from politics for over sixteen years. But his defiance lingers on:

> *A guy like me, when he sees a beautiful woman, he screws her, which is what I did. It happened. It was a passing incident in my life. It's over. I challenge any man not to have done the same.*

In 1978, it was the turn of another Canadian Cabinet Minister to face his peers. Francis Fox, a thirty-eight-year old Rhodes Scholar, was Canada's top law officer, when he rose, like Profumo, in the House of Commons:

A few years ago, before I entered the Cabinet, I was involved in a brief liaison with a married woman who became pregnant.

She subsequently applied for and secured the required permission for a therapeutic abortion.

On her admission to the hospital, I signed the name of her husband to an admitting document. . . .

I leave the Office of the Solicitor General of Canada in circumstances which I greatly regret, but with the hope that the Ministry and its agencies have been well-served during my tenure.

Neither the woman for whom Fox obtained the abortion, nor the author of the accusing letter that sparked his resignation have ever been identified. Fox was in tears as he left the House. Yet a year later, in the general election of 1979, he was able to maintain his seat in parliament.

Far too often, a politician's farewell is the unadorned truth:

I have been very shabbily treated, very shabbily. I am not a rootless phenomenon. I have done no harm to this country.
> Zulfikar Ali Bhutto, former Prime Minister
> of Pakistan, on his condemnation to death for the
> murder of a political opponent.

In politics, there are no thank you's.
> Dr. Morton Shulman, controversial member
> of the Ontario Legislature, on his intention to retire
> from public life.

The collective judgement of the people must be respected. My colleagues and I accept their verdict unreservedly in a spirit of humility.
> Indira Gandhi, following her defeat
> as Prime Minister of India.

Every word that boy said is the truth. I'm not fit for office!
> Claude Rains, as a senior U.S. Senate member
> in the film, *Mr. Smith Goes to Washington*, starring
> Jimmy Stewart.

'Five years are sufficient,' I said. 'It is beyond my strength to continue carrying this burden. I don't belong to any circle or faction within the party. I have only a circle of one to consult — myself. And this time my decision is final — irrevocable. I beg of you not to try to persuade me to change my mind for any reason at all. It will not help.'
> Golda Meir, Prime Minister of Israel,
> from her autobiography, *My Life*.

For Mohammed Reza Pahlavi, the Shah of Iran, retreat from the revolutionaries brought forth a masterpiece of pride and overstatement. The Shah, interviewed six months before his overthrow, said:

Nobody can overthrow me. I have the support of 700,000 troops, all of the workers and most of the people. I have the power.

When the time came for him to literally fly for his life, the Shah claimed in the face of overwhelming evidence to the contrary:

I am going on an extended vacation.

Shah Pahlavi & Ayatollah Khomeini

He then took the control of his own Boeing 707, which also carried a dozen security guards and a staff of twenty-five. In a last-minute gesture of loyalty, two of his army's generals tried to stop him, saying, "Please don't go."

The Shah replied:

I have to. It is in the interest of this country.

He then waved goodbye with these words:

Don't worry. Everything will be all right.

For Ali Bhutto of Pakistan, escape was too late. He was imprisoned by his political opponents and waited for a year in the death cell to be hanged on April 4, 1979. He wrote his own epitaph:

A poet and a revolutionary — that is what I have been all these years and that is how I shall remain until the last breath is gone from my body.

Yet in all the dark ruthlessness of power, there is surely some light. Oliver Wendell Holmes, the distinguished member of the American Supreme Court for over fifty years, delivered the following farewell on the radio in 1931 on the occasion of his 90th birthday:

In this symposium, my part is only to sit in silence. To express one's feelings as the end draws near is too intimate a task.

But I must mention one thought that comes to me as a listener in. The riders in a race do not stop short when they reach the goal. There is a little finishing canter before coming to a standstill. There is time to hear the kind voices of friends and to say to oneself: The work is done. But just as one says that, the answer comes: 'The race is over, but the work never is done while the power to work remains. The canter that brings you to a standstill need not be only coming to rest. It cannot be, while you still live. For to live is to function. That is all there is to living.'

And so I end with a line from a Latin poet who uttered the message more than fifteen hundred years ago, 'Death plucks my ear and says: Live — I am coming.'

Let us break now for a lengthy visit to that palace of great goodbyes — Watergate. For never in the history of leave-taking have so many statesmen fallen so loudly and so far. From President Richard Nixon down to the lowliest burglar, bidding adieu to power filled the air for years after the event itself. By the painful end, an American President, two Attorneys-General, a handful of Cabinet Ministers, close to a dozen aides and numerous private eyes, ex-Marines and tape recorder salesmen ran for cover as the case opened wide around them. Little did the world know that a bungled break-in at the Democratic Party headquarters would usher in a new Golden Age for America — where the farewell artist reigned supreme, bringing new meaning to the meaningless excuse, the lame lament and most of all, the false ending.

Even a partial cast of characters and their initial denials must include these masterpieces of dismissal:

Certain elements may try to stretch this beyond what it is.
> Ronald Zeigler, the morning after
> the Watergate break-in.

It's a third-rate burglary attempt, not worthy of further White House comment.
> Ronald Zeigler, the week after the break in.

I've looked into the matter very thoroughly, and I am convinced that neither Mr. Colson nor anyone else at the White House had any knowledge of, nor participation in the deplorable incident at the Democratic National Committee.
> Ken Clawson, deputy director of communications
> at the White House.

The White House has no involvement whatever in this particular incident.
> Richard Nixon, June 22, 1973,
> his first public comment on the break-in.

But the prize for most long-winded denial goes to Nixon's long-toothed Attorney-General, John Mitchell:

> *The person involved is the proprietor of a private security agency which was employed by our committee months ago to assist in the installation of our security system. He has, as we understand it, a number of business clients and interests, and we have no knowledge of these relationships. We want to emphasize that this man and the other people involved were not operating on either our behalf or with our consent. There is no place in our campaign or in the democratic process for this type of activity, and we will not permit or condone it.*

It didn't take Mitchell long to say goodbye to Nixon's presidential campaign. After ordering an investigation into the break-in, as Attorney-General, he resigned from Nixon's re-election committee, as campaign manager. Why? Because his wife, Martha, insisted that he quit:

> *... to meet the one obligation which must come first: the happiness and welfare of my wife and daughter.*

In accepting Mitchell's decision, Nixon said he was:

> *... most appreciative of the sacrifice Martha and you have made to the service of the nation.*

One of Nixon's aides was suspicious of this logic. In a conversation with *The Washington Post,* he claimed:

> *A man like John Mitchell doesn't give up all that power for his wife.*

The man at the centre of all this resignation turned righteous, then coy, then angry at those who tested his honesty:

I condemn any attempts to cover up in this case, no matter who is involved.

Richard Nixon, April 17, 1973
in a television address.

I don't give a shit what happens. I want you all to stonewall it, let them plead the Fifth Amendment, cover up or anything else, if it'll save it — save the plan. That's the whole point. We're going to protect our people if we can.

Richard Nixon, March 23, 1973,
in a private conversation with Mitchell, Dean and
Haldeman.

You know, I always wondered about taping equipment, but I'm damn glad we have it, aren't you?

Nixon to Haldeman, April 23, 1973.

On and on the denials went until some of the world's most powerful public servants bowed out with as much pride and as little grace as their circumstances could dictate.

The first two to bid adieu were Nixon's top assistants, Robert Haldeman and John Ehrlichman:

There is apparently to be no interruption in the flood of stories arising from Watergate . . . it has become virtually impossible under these circumstances to carry on my regular duties in the White House. . . . I am convinced that, in due course, I will have the opportunity to clear up any allegations or implications or impropriety, but also to demonstrate that I have always met the high and exacting standards of integrity which you (Nixon) have so clearly and properly demanded of all who serve on the White House staff.

Haldeman

Regardless of the actual facts, I have been the target of public attack. . . . The appearance of integrity, which is as important as integrity itself, can be affected by repeated rumor, unfounded charges or implications and whatever else the media causes.

Ehrlichman

On April 30, 1973, Nixon addressed the nation, accepting the responsibility (although not the blame) for Watergate, as well as the resignations of Haldeman; Ehrlichman; his new Attorney-General, Richard Kleindienst; and John Dean, his White House Counsel, who blew the lid on Nixon.

He begins in classic Nixon style:

Today, in one of the most difficult decisions of my presidency, I accepted the resignations of two of my closest associates in the White House, Bob Haldeman and John Ehrlichman, two of the finest public servants it has been my privilege to know. . . .

Nixon carries on, splitting hairs, bobbing and weaving from the crisis that would soon reach his own door:

> *I want to stress that in accepting these resignations, I mean to leave no implication whatever of personal wrong-doing on their part, and I leave no suggestion tonight of implication on the part of others who have been charged in this matter.*
>
> *But in matters as sensitive as guarding the integrity of our democratic process, it is essential that not only rigorous legal and ethical standards be observed, but also that the public, you, have the total confidence that they are both being observed and enforced by those in authority and particularly by the President of the United States. They agreed with me that this move was necessary in order to restore that confidence. ...*

Kleindienst, less important, took less time to bid goodbye:

> *Because Attorney-General Kleindienst, through a distinguished public service, my personal friend for twenty years, with no personal involvement whatsoever in this matter, has been a close personal and professional associate of some of those who are involved in this case, he and I both felt that it was also necessary to name a new Attorney-General.*

John Dean, Nixon's Judas, drew a single sentence:

> *The Counsel to the President, John Dean, has also resigned.*

But if ever a prize was deserving in what must be the longest extended series of political goodbyes in history, that prize belongs to Richard Nixon himself, who has made a career of leaving the American public — and coming back.

Nixon made famous the maxim:

> *There is one thing solid and fundamental in politics. What is up today is down tomorrow.*

He paid for it dearly from the press.

In the 1952 Presidential election campaign, Nixon refused to resign as Eisenhower's Vice-Presidential candidate after it was revealed that Nixon had a secret campaign fund. His famous "Checkers" speech climaxed on a personal note that had considerably more style than content:

> *One other thing I should probably tell you, because if I don't, they'll be probably saying this about me too. We did get something, a gift after the election. A man down in Texas heard Pat mention on the radio the fact that our two youngters would like to have a dog. And*

believe it or not, the day before we left on this campaign, we got a message from Union Station in Baltimore saying they had a package for us.

We went down to get it. You know what it was? It was a little cocker spaniel dog in a crate that he sent all the way from Texas. Black and white and spotted. And our little girl, Tricia, the six-year old, named it Checkers. And you know, the kids love the dog, and I just want to say this right now, that regardless of what they say about it, we're gonna keep it.

Ten years later, Nixon lost the race for Governor of California. The morning after his defeat, he spoke to reporters, burned his bridges and seemingly sealed his own political fate forever:

Now that all the members of the press are so delighted that I have lost. . . . I believe Governor Brown has a heart, even though he believes that I do not. . . . I did not win. I have no hard feelings against anybody, against any opponent and least of all, the people of California.

. . . And as I leave the press, all I can say is this: For 16 years, ever since the Hiss case, you've had a lot of fun — a lot of fun — that you've had an opportunity to attack me. . . . Just think about how much you're going to be missing me.

You won't have Nixon to kick around any more, because, gentlemen, this is my last press conference.

As a stunned press corps filed their stories, Governor Brown summed up their feelings:

Nixon is going to regret all his life that he made that speech. The press will never let him forget it.

When Nixon finally did resign from politics on August 8th, 1974, his career was in ruins, but his eloquence lingered on. To the American people he bade a humble goodbye in which he ingeniously attempted to use the Watergate scandal in an effort to rescue his own integrity:

This is the thirty-seventh time I have spoken to you from this office in which so many decisions have been made that shape the history of the nation.

Each time I have done so to discuss with you some matters that I believe affected the national interest. And all the decisions I have made in my public life I have always tried to do what was best for the nation.

Throughout the long and difficult period of Watergate, I have felt it was my duty to persevere; to make every possible effort to complete the term of office to which you elected me.

In the past few days, however, it has become evident to me that I no longer have a strong enough political base in Congress to justify continuing that effort. . . .

I would have preferred to carry through to the finish whatever the personal agony it would have involved, and my family unanimously urged me to do so.

But the interests of the nation must always come before any personal considerations. From the discussions I have had with Congressional and other leaders I have concluded that because of the Watergate matter I might not have the support of the Congress that I would consider necessary to back the very difficult decisions and carry out the duties of this office in the way the interests of the nation will require.

I have never been a quitter.

To leave office before my term is completed is opposed to every instinct in my body. But as President I must put the interests of America first.

America needs a full-time President and a full-time Congress, particularly at this time with problems we face at home and abroad.

To continue to fight through the months ahead for my personal vindication would almost totally absorb the time and attention of both the President and Congress in a period when our entire focus should be on the great issues of peace abroad and prosperity without inflation at home.

Therefore, I shall resign the Presidency effective at noon tomorrow.

Vice President Ford will be sworn in as President at that hour in this office.

To the White House staff, he said this in a tearful and highly ironic farewell address:

Always give your best. Never get discouraged. Never be petty. Always remember; others may hate you. Those who hate you don't win unless you hate them. And then you destroy yourself. . . .

Only if you have been in the deepest valley can you ever know how magnificent it is to be on the highest mountain.

Nixon then boarded an Army helicopter, and raised his arms one last time in his familiar V-for-Victory gesture.

The final word on Watergate belongs not to Nixon but to Gerald R. Ford, the man who took office to succeed him, and in so doing, to pardon him:

... There are no historic or legal precedents to which I can turn in this matter, none that precisely fit the circumstances of a private citizen who has resigned the Presidency of the United States. But it is common knowledge that serious allegations and accusations hang like a sword over our former President's head, and threaten his health as he tries to reshape his life. ... Many months and perhaps more years will have to pass before Richard Nixon could hope to obtain a fair trial by jury in any jurisdiction of the United States. ... But it is not the ultimate fate of Richard Nixon that most concerns me ... but the immediate future of this great country. ... Finally, I feel that Richard Nixon and his loved ones have suffered enough, and will continue to suffer no matter what I do, no matter what we as a great and good nation can do together to make his goal of peace come true. ...

Now, therefore, I, Gerald R. Ford, President of the United States ... have granted and do grant a full, free and absolute pardon unto Richard Nixon for all offenses against the United States which he ... has committed or may have committed or taken part in during the period from January 20, 1969 through August 9, 1974.

Not all America's political goodbyes are surrounded by corruption. What is extraordinary about the United States is that two of its most critical moments in history took the form of a farewell.

One was the Declaration of Independence in which America bid farewell to the colonizing influence of England and opened the door to self-rule:

When in the Course of human events it becomes necessary for one people to dissolve the political bands which have connected them with another, and to assume among the powers of the earth, the separate and equal station to which the Laws of Nature and of Nature's God entitle them, a decent respect to the opinions of mankind requires that they should declare the causes which impel them to this separation. ...

We ... declare that these United Colonies are and of right ought to be free and independent states; that they are absolved from all allegiance to the British Crown, and that all political connections between them and the State of Great Britain, is and ought to be totally dissolved. ...

The other was Abraham Lincoln's Gettysburg Address, which provided one of the most stirring eulogies to the American ideal:

Four score and seven years ago our fathers brought forth on this continent, a new nation, conceived in liberty, and dedicated to the proposition that all men are created equal.

Now we are engaged in a great civil war, testing whether that nation, or any nation so conceived and so dedicated can long endure. We are met on a great battlefield of that war. We have come to dedicate a portion of that field, as a final resting place for those who here gave their lives that that nation might live. It is altogether fitting and proper, that we should do this.

But, in a larger sense, we cannot dedicate — we cannot consecrate — we cannot hallow this ground. The brave men, living and dead, who struggled here, have consecrated it far above our poor power to add or detract. The world will little note, nor long remember what we say here, but it can never forget what they did here.

It is for us, the living, rather, to be dedicated here to the unfinished work which they who have fought here have thus far so nobly advanced. It is rather for us to be here dedicated to the great task remaining before us — that from these honoured dead we take the increased devotion to that cause for which they gave the last full measure of devotion — that we here highly resolve that these dead shall not have died in vain — that this nation, under God, shall have a new birth of freedom — and that government of the people, by the people, for the people, shall not perish from the earth.

Lest we think that such stirring sentiments went universally unchallanged, the *Chicago Times* observed that the Address was:

. . . an offensive exhibition of boorishness and vulgarity. . . . puerile, not alone in literary construction, but in its ideas, its sentiments, its grasp. . . . By the side of it, mediocrity is superb.

Lincoln was shot dead on April 14, 1865, at Ford's Theatre in Washington. His assassin, John Wilkes Booth, said this on his way to the gallows:

Our country owes all her troubles to him, and God simply made me the instrument of his punishment.

Ironically, Lincoln had written in what turned out to be his Will:

I have all my life been a fatalist. What is to be, will be, or rather, I have found all my life as Hamlet says: 'There is a divinity that shapes our ends, rough-hew them how we will.'

If unity has been an abiding strength of the American people, the excuse of national unity has been used by Presidents and scoundrels alike (especially when they are both!) to leave office with their honor intact. After losing immense popularity over the Vietnam War, Lyndon Johnson put his tenure plainly in a television address on March 31, 1968, in which he announced a partial halt to the bombing of North Vietnam:

This country's ultimate strength lies in the unity of our people. There is division in the American House now. There is divisiveness among us all tonight. And holding the trust that is mine, as President of all the people, I cannot disregard the peril to the progress of the American people and the hope and the prospect of peace for all people. . . . With America's sons in the fields far away, with America's future under challenge right here at home . . . I do not believe I should devote an hour or a day of my time to any personal partisan causes. . . . Accordingly, I shall not seek, and will not accept the nomination of my Party for another term as your President.

Not all American Presidents have been forced to resign (although the three President's of the 1960's all had their terms cut short). On occasion, the Chief of State has done honor to his office:

Though, in reviewing the incidents of my administration, I am unconscious of intentional error, I am, nevertheless, too sensible of my defects not to think it probable that I may have committed many errors. . . .

George Washington

Washington continued his hour-long address to the newly-formed Congress, and concluded with a single sentence that seems never to end. Take a deep breath:

Relying on its (Congress) kindness in this, as in other things, and actuated by that fervent love towards it, which is so natural to a man who views it in the native soil of himself and his progenitors for several generations, I anticipate, with pleasing expectations, that retreat in which I promise myself to realize, without alloy, the sweet enjoyment of partaking, in the midst of my fellow citizens, the benign influence of good laws under a free government — the ever-favourite object of my heart, and the happy reward, as I trust, of our mutual cares, labours and dangers.

Franklin Roosevelt died in his office of a cerebral hemorrhage. Five weeks earlier, he spoke to Congress for the last time, following his meeting with Stalin and Churchill at Yalta. It was the last time he had delivered a major speech standing up, and the first time any President addressed Congress sitting down:

I hope that you will pardon me for the unusual posture of sitting down. . . . It makes it a lot easier for me not to have to carry about ten pounds of steel on the bottom of my legs.

While having his portrait painted on April 12, 1945, Roosevelt called out:

I have a terrible headache.

He slumped back into his chair, unconscious, and died.

Yet the most ironic Presidential goodbye belongs to Robert Kennedy. In 1967, he uttered these words that would turn to dust a year later with his own assassination:

> *Who knows whether any of us will be around in 1972? Existence is so fickle, fate so fickle.*

Even before this, his sister-in-law, Jacqueline Kennedy pronounced the following eulogy on her own dead husband, John Fitzgerald Kennedy:

> *Now I think that I should have known that he was* magic *all along. I did know it — but I should have guessed that it would be too much to ask to grow old with him and see our children grow up together . . . so now he is a legend when he would have preferred to be a man.*

Lest you think that a politician's farewells must always be coupled with embarrassment, shame and criminal prosecution, remember that the oratory of leave-taking has reached equal and opposite heights of distinction. When Karl Marx died in 1883 and was buried in London's Highgate Cemetary, his great friend, Frederic Engels, said this over his grave:

> *On the afternoon of the 14th of March, at a quarter to three, the greatest living thinker ceased to think. . . . It is impossible to measure the loss which the fighting European and American proletariat and historical science have lost with the death of this man. . . . As Darwin discovered the laws of evolution in organic nature, so Marx described the law of evolution in human history, the simple fact that human beings eat, drink, shelter and clothe themselves before they can turn their attention to politics, science, art and religion. . . .*

Winston Churchill laughed in the face of death, as he foretold his readiness for it:

> *I am ready to meet my Maker. Whether my Maker is prepared for the great ordeal of meeting me is another matter.*

Death, in fact, has a way of creeping into political farewells of all kinds:

> *People only leave by way of the box — ballot or coffin.*
> U.S. Senator Claiborne Pell

> *Come in and have some fried post-mortems on toast.*
> Adlai Stevenson, the morning after losing
his bid for the American Presidency, 1952.

> *All political parties die, at last, of swallowing their own lies.*
> John Arbuthnot, physician to the Court of Queen
Anne.

This desk of mine is one at which a man may die, but from which he cannot resign.

President Dwight D. Eisenhower, many years before
his Vice-President, Richard Nixon, did resign.

The work was killing me; they called me out of bed at all hours of the night to receive resignations of prime ministers.

Vincent Aurid, on his retirement as
President of France, 1954.

I have tried my best to give the nation everything I had in me. There are probably a million people who could have done this job better than I did it, but I had the job and I always quote an epitaph on a tombstone in a cemetery in Tombstone, Arizona: 'Here lies Jack Williams. He done his damndest.'

Harry S. Truman, on his resignation as
President of the U.S.

It was Truman also who said goodbye to faint-hearted associates with a phrase that has entered the language: "If you can't stand the heat, get out of the kitchen."

Some who chose to resign from the heat did so like this:

I'm sure there will be those who will be able to contain their regret without difficulty but I have been under no pressure whatsoever.

Paul Warnke, the United States' chief arms negotiator,
on his resignation in 1978. Congress had accused him
of being too soft with the Soviet Union.

Jack Gilligan and I are great friends and remain so. But we have disagreements over the management and policies of development assistance. Therefore, I think that it is better that he find someone else more in agreement with his own outlook.

Frederick Van Dyke politely resigns as
assistant administrator of Jimmy Carter's
Agency for International Development.

It is important that my name and reputation be cleared. For me, my wife, my children and grand children, and those who have faith in me. As I said in Senate hearings, my conscience is clear.

Bert Lance, who resigned as U.S. Budget Director,
after a bitter dispute over his personal finances. His
friend Jimmy Carter defended Lance by saying:
"He's a good man."

Never murder a man who is committing suicide.

Woodrow Wilson on the election of a
state Governor he clearly despised.

Dean Acheson, the distinguished U.S. Secretary of State, exited with considerably more grace:

I will undoubtedly have to seek what is happily known as gainful employment, which I am glad to say does not describe holding public office.

Occasionally, contradiction creeps into resignation. When Dwight Eisenhower was thinking of not running for a second Presidential term, one of his critics facetiously told why:

It was then that he faced the sheer godawful boredom of not being President.

Yet when it was all over for Ike in 1969, he looked forward to retirement with sheer joy, saying:

Ah, that lovely title, ex-President.

Herbert Hoover was much more bitter about the prospect of his own retirement, claiming it is a time

When one shrivels up into a nuisance for all mankind.

One of the nastiest series of farewells belongs to Kaiser Wilhelm II of Germany. He was the ultimate Prussian soldier and took great glee in addressing anyone who stood near him with lengthy harangues on whatever entered his mind. When some of his troops were slaughtered in the Boxer Rebellion of 1900, the Kaiser gave countless farewells to his armies who were sent off to avenge the Chinese. Three times within a single month, he addressed his troups in language that shocked the diplomatic courts of Europe:

The German flag has been outraged and the German empire has been insulted. That demands exemplary reparation and vengeance.... You will face death with an army who defies death no less than you do.... You are to fight against a cunning, courageous, well-armed and cruel foe. When you are upon him, know this: spare nobody, take no prisoners.... Recently, the enemy has fought bravely, a fact which has not yet been sufficiently explained.

Yet like so many commanders-in-chief, Wilhelm had a harder time welcoming his troops home than bidding them farewell:

You will be home before the leaves have fallen from the trees.
Kaiser Wilhem II, addressing his tropps
leaving for the front, August 1914.

I have told you once and I will tell you again — your boys will not be sent into any foreign wars.
Franklin D. Roosevelt,
in an election speech, 1940.

Your boys will be home for Christmas.
Richard Nixon, 1971.

Generals are as bad at resigning as Princes and Presidents. But General MacArthur did it by addressing the American Congress after being fired by President Truman following a disagreement over the war in Korea:

> *The world has turned over many times since I took the oath on the plain at West Point, and the hopes and dreams have long since vanished. But I still remember the refrain of one of the most popular barracks ballads of that day which proclaimed most proudly that old soldiers never die; they just fade away.*
>
> *But like the old soldiers of that ballad, I now close my military career and just fade away, an old soldier who tried to do his duty as God gave him the light to see that duty. Good-by.*

MacArthur's poignancy was balanced by Churchill's irony on leaving office. Writing in 1946, he summed up his feelings about being defeated at the polls in the first post-War elections:

Winston Spencer Churchill

Then, on the 10th of May, 1940, at the outset of this mighty battle, I acquired the chief power in the state, which henceforth I wielded in ever-growing measure for five years and three months of world war, all our enemies having surrendered unconditionally, or being about to do so, I was immediately dismissed by the British electorate from all conduct of their affairs.

Churchill ended W.W. II the way his unfortunate predecessor began it. Neville Chamberlain had flown to Germany twice in 1938 and returned with reassurances from Hitler that Europe wouldn't be turned into a battleground. While Hitler bid farewell to peace:

National Socialism (Naziism) does not harbor the slightest agressive intent towards any European nation.

Chamberlain first reassured his people, then saw them turn him from office.

Addressing a crowd of grateful supporters outside 10 Downing Street, he said:

My good friends, this is the second time in our history that there has come back from Germany to Downing Street peace with honour. . . . I belive it is peace for our time. We thank you from the bottom of our hearts. And now, I recommend you to go home and sleep quietly in your beds.

A few months later, Hitler had made a mockery of these words. The task of ousting Chamberlain fell to Lloyd George, still a member of the House, and the Prime Minister during the previous World War:

He appealed for sacrifice from the nation. The nation is ready as its leadership is right, as long as you can say clearly what you are aiming at, as long as you can give confidence to them that their leaders are doing their best for them.

I say now solemnly that the Prime Minister can give an example of sacrifice because I tell him one thing, that there is nothing that would contribute more to victory in this war than that he should sacrifice his seals of office.

One of England's greatest orators, Edmund Burke, also found himself thrown out of office. He sought to explain his controversial policies in the House of Commons to his constituents in Bristol, and offered to resign while remaining in the race for his seat:

I am not come by a false and counterfeit show of deference to seduce in my favour. I ask it seriously and unaffectedly. If you wish that I should retire, I shall not consider that advice as a censure upon my conduct, or an alteration in your sentiments, but as a rational submission to the circumstances of affairs.

But after a week of canvassing his neighbors, he decided his fight to remain in office was hopeless, and he withdrew:

Gentlemen: I decline the election. . . . I have not canvassed the whole of this city in form. But I have taken such a view of it as satisfies my own mind that your choice will ultimately not fall on me. . . . I am not in the least surprised, nor in the least angry at this view of things. I have read the book of life for a long time, and I have read other books a little. Nothing has happened to me but what has happened to men much better than me.

The most touching and eloquent address to constituents belongs, however, to Abraham Lincoln, who bid his hometown farewell after being elected President of the United States:

No one not in my situation, can appreciate my feeling of sadness at this parting. To this place and the kindess of these people, I owe everything. Here I have lived a quarter of a century, and have passed from a young man to an old man. Here my children have been born and one is buried.

I now leave, not knowing whether ever I may return, with a task before me greater than that which rested upon Washington. Without the assistance of that Divine Being who attended him, I cannot succeed. With that assistance, I cannot fail.

Trusting in him who can go with me, and remain with you, and be everywhere for good, let us confidently hope that all will yet be good. To his care commending you, as I hope in your prayers you will commend me, I bid you an affectionate farewell.

Lincoln then left for Washington, from which he never returned. A similar fate met another American President, James Garfield, who was also assassinated. His great friend, James G. Blain, paid tacit homage to them both:

For the second time in this generation, the great departments of the government of the United States are assembled in the Hall of Representatives to do honor to the memory of a murdered President. Garfield was slain in a day of peace. . . . Great in life, he was surpassingly great in death. For no cause, in the very frenzy of wantonness and wickedness by the red hand of murder, he was thrust from the full tide of the world's interests. . . . Help us believe that in the silence of the receding world he heard the great waves breaking on a further shore and felt already upon his wasted brow the breath of the eternal morning.

The farewell of civil war is perhaps the saddest of all, and from across the continents, two great statesmen, Mirabeau and Jefferson, each served notice on their governments that their days were numbered. Haranguing a doddering and corrupt French Assembly, Mirabeau warned them of the Revolution to come:

> *In all countries, in all ages, have aristocrats implacably pursued the friends of the people. . . . But you, Commons, listen to one who, unseduced by your applause, yet cherishes them in his heart. . . . No measure of outrage shall bear down on my patience. I have been, I am, I shall be, even to the tomb, the man of the public liberty, the man of the constitution. If to be such to become the man of the people rather than of the nobles, then woe to the privileged orders! For privilege shall have an end, but the people is eternal!*

The last word on political goodbyes is reserved for Thomas Jefferson, who slowly, carefully and elegantly informed his colleagues in the Congress that the state of Mississippi which he represented was leaving the Union:

> *I rise, Mr. President, for the purpose of announcing to the Senate that the state of Mississippi . . . has declared her separation from the United States. Under these circumstances, of course, my functions are terminated here. . . . Whatever offense I have given which has not been redressed, or for which satisfaction has not been demanded, I have, Senators, in this hour of parting, to offer you my apology for any pain which in the heat of discourse I have inflicted. I go hence unencumbered of the remembrance of an injury received, and having discharged the duty of making the only reparation in my power for an injury offered.*

Part Three

*Do not go gentle into
that good night.*

Chapter 5

"If this is dying, I don't think much of it."
Lytton Strachey

Oscar Wilde called it the one thing no one can survive. If you forget about taxes for a moment, death is the only inevitability left. This in turn has led us to utter some profound and often absurd pronouncements on the subject. In 1658 Sir Thomas Browne said that the long habit of living indisposes us for dying. In our own century, Woody Allen has said that it is impossible to experience one's own death and still carry a tune. The fact is that few of us are willing to cross the line without a good excuse, a choice remark, a plea for mercy, a swift executioner or a forgiving public to immortalize our last breath.

The entire subject of the final goodbye was put in its proper — if long-winded — perspective by Walt Whitman:

> *Last words are not samples of the best which involve vitality at its full, and balance and perfect control and scope. But they are valuable beyond measure to confirm and endorse the varied train, facts, theories and faith of the whole preceding life.*

Karl Marx differed radically. In a conversation with his housekeeper the day he died, the following drama took place:

HELEN: *Tell me your last words, Karl. I'll write them down.*
MARX: *You can hardly spell your own name!*
HELEN: *Your last word to all mankind. . . ?*
MARX: *I haven't got one.*
HELEN: *Your dying breath, so I can put it in all those big fat books — like Words on Their Deathbeds The Great Men Said. Come along Karl, think!"*
MARX: *Go on, get out. Last words are for fools who haven't said enough!*

Shakespeare said more, with less:

> *Oh, but they say the tongues of dying men*
> *Enforce the attention like deep harmony.*
>
> Shakespeare, Richard II.

Yet the evidence of last words as final goodbyes would seem to be weighted against Marx and more in favor of Shakespeare. John Irving's fictional character T. S. Garp had given considerable care and thought to his own last words. After his death, his wife, Helen, found a note instructing her to say that no matter what his last words actually were she should say they were these:

> *I have always known that the pursuit of excellence is a lethal habit.*

Dominique Bonhours, a nineteenth century grammarian, displayed an acute presence of mind on his deathbed, remaining a grammarian to the last:

> *I am about to — or I am going to — die.*
> *Either expression is used.*

Others have managed to be a little more blasé about the whole thing. Bernard Shaw was realistic about his own death. To his nurse he said:

> *Sister, you are trying to keep me alive as an old curiosity. But I'm done. I'm finished. I'm going to die.*

The English economist and biographer, Lytton Strachey, was indifferent:

> *If this is dying, I don't think much of it.*

... while Thomas Carlyle muttered:

> *So this is death, is it? Well...*

... and Lord Palmerston said:

> *Die, my dear doctor; that's the last thing I shall do.*

If you have to die of a severe, continual hiccup, as the Scottish poet James Hogg did, what else could you say but:

> *It is a reproach to the Faculty that they cannot cure the hiccup.*

Yet for some people, the final goodbye is nothing more than a journey home:

> *Well, I'm all packed and ready to go. I'm an aged agnostic, unafraid of death and undeluded with thoughts of a life hereafter.*
>
> Gregory Clark, Canadian journalist, at age 82.

For more than 900 Americans who left their home to join a religious fanatic called the Rev. Jim Jones, death came in the jungles of Guyana with these comforting words from the man who engineered the largest mass suicide the world has witnessed:

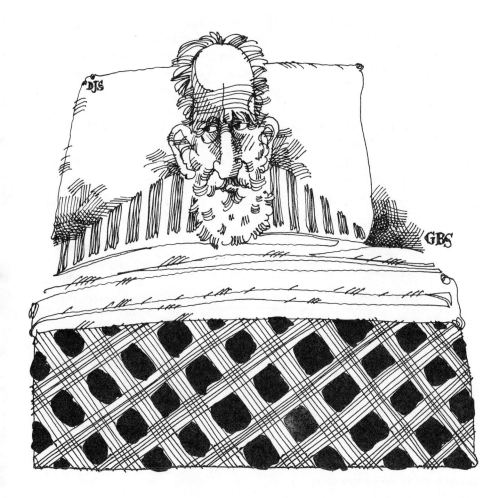

What's going to happen here in a matter of a few minutes is that one of those people in the plane is going to shoot the pilot. . . . So you be kind to the children and be kind to seniors, and take the potion like they used to in Ancient Greece, and step over quietly, because we are not committing suicide — it's a revolutionary act.

Everybody dies. I haven't seen anybody yet didn't die. And I like to choose my own kind of death for a change. I'm tired of being tormented to hell. Tired of it. (Applause)

A few cultists protested. Some women screamed. Children cried. Armed guards took up positions around the camp to keep anyone from escaping:

Let the little children in and reassure them. . . . They're not crying from pain, it's just a little bitter-tasting. . . . Death is a million times more preferable to spend more days in this life. If you knew what was ahead of you, you'd be glad to be stepping over tonight . . . quickly, quickly, no more pain. . . . This world was not your home. . . .

Here the tape runs out. The sound stops before the report of the pistol that killed Jim Jones, presumably fired by his own hand.

The sense of "stepping over" from this world to the next is repeated throughout history:

When you come to the hedge that we must all go over, it isn't bad. You feel sleepy and you don't care. Jut a little dreamy anxiety about which world you're really in, that's all.
Stephen Crane.

Even going my journey; they have greased my boots already.
Rabelais.

Now I am about to take my last voyage, a great leap in the dark.
Thomas Hobbes, 1679.

Agnes, Darling: If such should be we never meet again, while firing my last shot, I will gently breathe the name of my wife — Agnes — and with wishes even for my enemies, I will make the plunge and try to swim to the other shore.
Wild Bill Hickock in a letter to his wife.

We are all over the hill, we shall go better now.
Frederick the Great

Such relaxed sanity sounds comforting years after the fact. But the sad truth is that many people — even well-known people — meet their maker with considerably less *sang-froid*.

The French novelist, Honore de Balzac, looked up at his doctor and cried out:

Send for Bianchon! He'll save me!

Unfortunately, Dr. Bianchon was one of Balzac's own characters from his masterwork, *La Comedie Humaine*. Apparently, Balzac had always found his fictional characters to have greater presence than his real life contemporaries.

Charles IX of France panicked at the end:

Nurse, nurse, what murder, what blood!
Oh, I have done wrong. God, pardon me!

Elias Baldwin, a gambler, fought on in vain:

By gad, I'm not licked yet!

And Washington Irving sought to hasten his death:

> *Well, I must arrange my pillows for another weary night! When will this end?*

To some participants, death is less than exciting. Having led a tempestuous and full life, Winston Churchill understandably found death to be a tiresome business. He merely said.

> *I am bored with it all.*

And Lord Byron, who led an equally exciting if somewhat more exotic life, retired with the words:

> *I want to go to sleep now.*

Others have been quite stoic in the face of their own mortality. Accepting death as part of the natural course of events, they wish to have done with it:

> *Well — if we must, we must — and in that case the less said the better.*
>
> Richard Brinsley Sheridan

> *I'd rather live, but I am not afraid to die.*
>
> Benjamin Disraeli

> *I were miserable if I might not die. . . .*
> *Thy kingdom come, Thy will be done.*
>
> John Donne

> *It is not my design to drink or sleep, but to make what haste I can to be gone.*
>
> Oliver Cromwell

> *Get it done more quickly.*
>
> George Grant, principal of Queen's University in Canada.

> *Let me have my own fidgets.*
>
> Walter Bagehot

> *This is the last of earth. I am content.*
>
> John Quincy Adams

America's first President, George Washington, faced death stoically:

> *Doctor, I die hard, but I am not afraid to go.*

North of the border, Canadian Prime Ministers had fewer words, presumably for fewer people:

> *It's the end.*
>
> Sir Wilfred Laurier

> *Thank you.*
>
> Mackenzie King

For some people, it's a matter of light and death; of ups and downs. Geothe cried out on his deathbed:

More light!

For Marie Louise, Empress of France, light was essential:

I will not sleep; I wish to meet death wide awake.

Jean Jacques Rousseau said:

I go to see the sun for the last time.

Theodore Roosevelt's dying words were:

Please put out the lights.

G. K. Chesterton put the matter of light and death more succinctly:

The issue is now clear. It is between light and darkness and everyone must choose his side.

The Chinese philosopher, Chuang Tzu, in calming the fears of his followers who felt the buzzards would eat his body, said:

Above ground, I shall be food for kites (birds); below ground, I shall be food for mole-crickets and ants. Why rob one to feed the other?

Since death is the experience we fear most in life, it is not unnatural that our final words would reflect that unease about facing the final breath. Despite the obvious inconvenience of dying, many people have greeted it with a mixture of indifference, expectation and, occasionally, ecstasy:

This is the best of all possible worlds.

Arthur Brisbane, journalist.

So here it is at last, the distinguished thing.

Henry James

From my present sensations, I should say I was dying — and I am glad of it.

George Combe

I am not the least afraid to die.

Charles Darwin

I know that all things on earth must have an end, and I have come to mine.

Sir Joshua Reynolds

John Keats' tragic death at the age of twenty-six cut short a brilliant poetical career. Like his brother, whom he had nursed through death a few years earlier, Keats died of consumption. During the last agonizing moments of his life he said to his friend, the painter Joseph Severn:

Lift me up, for I am dying. I shall die easy. Don't be frightened. Thank God it has come!

Keats had earlier said goodbye to another friend, Charles Armitage Brown, in a letter written a few months before his death:

> *I can scarcely bid you good-bye, even in a letter. I always made an awkward bow. God bless you!*

The American diarist, Marie Bashkirtseff, on seeing the candle by her bed burnt almost to its socket, said:

> *We shall go out together.*

But when Oscar Wilde was presented with a similar fate at his own bedside, he chose to address his new curtains:

> *Either they go, or I do.*

He did.

Very often, final goodbyes to the world are made in all innocence. In these cases death is not predictable and comes as a complete surprise. Albert, King of Belgium, gave the following instructions to some traveling companions:

> *Follow the path for another fifty yards. I am going back to the foot of the rocks to make another climb. If I feel in good form, I shall take the difficult way up; if I do not, I shall take the easy one. I shall join you in an hour.*

He didn't, but fell to his death from the mountain.

Novelist Donn Byrne was killed in an automobile accident that followed these words:

> *I think I'll go for a drive before dinner. Anyone coming along?*

The Earl of Godwin was accused by Edward the Confessor of murdering his brother. In protesting his innocence, Godwin said this . . .

> *So might I safely swallow this morsel of bread, as I am guiltless of this deed.*

. . . and promptly choked to death.

Denis Diderot took an apricot after his wife pleaded that he needed the nourishment:

> *But what the devil do you think this will do to me?*

It killed him instantly.

Anthony Drexel III, of the famous banking family, was showing friends his souvenir pistols, when he said:

> *Here's one you've never seen before!*

. . . and accidentally shot himself.

And Robert, Lord Clive, when asked by a lady if he would make her a pen, took out a small knife and said:

To be sure!

Much to the disconcerted lady's surprise, Clive then killed himself with his own knife.

Lawrence Oates, on the other hand, knew full well that he was committing suicide. A member of the ill-fated Scott expedition, Oates was overcome with frostbite and depression. Judging himself to be an unnecessary burden on the other members of the expedition, Oates walked out of the base-tent with the words:

I am just going out and may be some time.

He never returned.

Death has many entrances and exits. Sometimes, as we shall observe in the next chapter, it enters dramatically amid fanfare and ritual; or, as in the passages we have just seen, it enters in an ironic fashion, stealing its victim in a wholly unexpected manner. At other times, death walks on slippered feet, and the end comes quietly, peacefully, resignedly. D. H. Lawrence once wrote:

Death is the only pure, beautiful conclusion of a great passion.

He died in 1930 of pleurisy, but not before his final words:

I am better now.

Death was greeted with a similar nonchalance by the industrialist Alfred I. Du Pont, whose last words were:

Thank you, doctors. Thank you, nurses. I'll be all right in a few days.

Lewis Carroll died with this command:

Take away those pillows. I shall need them no more.

He was quite right.

Cyrus the Great was clearly a man of many last words:

And now, it seems to me that my life begins to ebb; I feel my spirit slipping away from those parts she leaves the first. If you would take my hand once more, draw near me now; but when I have covered my face, let no man look upon me again, not even you, my sons.

The poet Robert Browning passed on after hearing that his play,*Asolando,* was nearly sold out, with the final exclamation:

How gratifying.

Katherine Mansfield said:

I believe I am going to die.

Samuel Johnson had no doubt about it:

I am about to die.

And Rabelais was not so sure:

I am going to seek the great perhaps.

Louis Riel, the Métis leader who was sentenced to hang by the Canadian government in 1885, held the courtroom enraptured with his defense. But on the day of his execution he told a journalist this:

Every day in which I have neglected to prepare myself to die, was a day of mental alienation.

Another Canadian (Riel despised the term), the Quebec reformer Sir Louis-Hippolyte Lafontaine, died with a message for what lay ahead — and below:

J'aime mon Dieu, et j'aime mon Pays.

The most understated assessment of the difference between life and death comes from the English writer Leigh Hunt, whose last words were:

I don't think I shall ever get over this.

Mark Twain was not optimistic about the human condition — even when it ends:

Whoever has lived long enough to find out what life is, knows how deep a debt of gratitude we owe to Adam, the first great benefactor of our race. He brought death into the world.

Twain's own death came as somewhat of a surprise to the great humorist, especially as he was alive to read about it. He had become the unwitting victim of a careless journalist who had composed a premature obituary notice. Mr. Twain was not amused, and his reply lives on as a masterpiece of rebuttal:

Rumours of my death are greatly exaggerated.

Andrew Bonar Law, Prime Minister of Great Britain, died murmuring this strange phrase to his attendant:

You are a curious fellow.

As the news of the world was read to Stopford Brooke on his deathbed, the man of letters replied:

It will be a pity to leave all that.

Three of the cheeriest goodbyes belong to women. Asked in her final seconds if she wanted anything, Jane Austen replied:

Nothing but death.

When Elizabeth Barrett Browning was asked how she felt, she whispered:

Beautiful!

Emily Dickinson passed on with these mystical words:

I must go in, the fog is rising.

For Charlotte Brontë, the end was not so peaceful. To her new husband of three months, she cried:

Oh, I am not going to die, am I? He will not separate us, we have been so happy.

For James Joyce, whose prose baffled critics and readers alike, death held but one question:

Does nobody understand?

Although death and its dignity have been chronicled in countless books, occasionally the authors themselves have faced the finality with less grace than style. This was certainly the case with the literary couple whose lives bordered on fiction. Writing shortly before F. Scott Fitzgerald's death in 1941, his wife Zelda penned these damning words to him:

Your entire life will soon be accounted for by the toils we have so assiduously woven — your leisure is eaten by habits of leisure, your money by habitual extravagance, your hope by cynicism and mine by frustration, your ambition by too much dissipation.

When Scott Fitzgerald died, it was at the home of another woman, the Hollywood gossip columnist Sheilah Graham. The author of *The Great Gatsby* and *The Last Tycoon* gave as he got with Zelda, but reached a separate peace with Graham:

I want something sweet, I'm going to Schwab's for some ice cream.

Graham handed him a Hershey bar instead. Savoring it, he started writing the nicknames of the football heroes of his class beside their names in the *Princeton Alumni Weekly*. . . .

Zelda died alone and wordless in a fire that engulfed the Alabama mental institution to which she had been committed.

Fitzgerald's literary counterpart and counter-puncher was Ernest Hemingway, who in his novels brought a quiet poignancy to the facts of death that made his own suicide with a shotgun especially appalling. In this famous final scene from *A Farewell to Arms,* the understatement is deafening:

The nurse opened her door and motioned with her finger for me to come. I followed her into the room. Catherine did not look up when I came in. I went over to the side of the bed. The doctor was standing by the bed on the opposite side. Catherine looked at me and smiled. I bent down over the bed and started to cry.

"Poor darling," Catherine said softly. She looked grey.

"You're all right, Cat," I said. "You're going to be all right."

"I'm going to die," she said; then waited and said, "I hate it."

. . . . .

I waited outside the hall. I waited a long time. The nurse came to the door and came over to me. "I'm afraid Mrs. Henry is very ill," she said. "I'm afraid for her."

"Is she dead?"

"No, but she is unconscious."

It seems she had one hemorrhage after another. They couldn't stop it. I went into the room and stayed with Catherine until she died. She was unconscious all the time, and it did not take very long for her to die.

Hemingway's own death was nasty, brutal and short. From a newspaper account of his suicide in Ketchum, Idaho, we hear this conversation with his wife, Mary:

MARY: [*singing an old Haleas' folksong while undressing for bed in her room*] *Tutti, mi chiamono bionda. Ma bionda io non soro.*

ERNEST: [*joins in the next phrase; singing loudly
    from his room*] *Porto capelli neri.*
 MARY: *Good night, my lamb. Sleep well.*
ERNEST: *Good night, my kitten.*

The next morning, Mary heard two loud bangs, and rushed downstairs to
find Ernest dead.

Chapter 6

"I have had just about all I can take of myself."
S. N. Behrman

If Hemingway was a pragmatist who took his own life, many others have managed to endure death without pulling the trigger on themselves:

I will tell you this: when the end is on its way, no amount of noise will help. If you get noisy, you lose face with yourself.
Lillian Hellman

When you must go, then go. And make as little fuss as you can.
Tao-Chien

Why do you weep? Do you think I should live forever? I thought dying would have been more difficult.
Louis XV to his servants.

There are men I could spend eternity with, but not this life.
Kathleen Norris

By understanding many things, I have accomplished nothing.
Hugo Grotius

The cost of living is seeing others die.
Abraham L. Feinberg,
Toronto Rabbi.

For the Irish playwright, Sean O'Casey, death came along after these final words that he chose for the autobiography that he completed at the age of seventy:

Here, with whitened hair, desire failing, strength ebbing out of him, the sun gone down and with only the serenity and the calm waning of the evening star left to him, he drank to Life, to all that had been, to what it was, to what it would be. Hurrah!

Forcing one's own goodbye early on is a time-honored, though often dishonorable end to the world. In many countries attempting suicide is a crime, punishable by imprisonment. Yet from the words of those who have met death at their own hands, the jury is still out on how strongly we should judge them. The American philosopher, Willam James, called suicide:

The naturally consistent course dictated by the logical intellect.

Albert Camus said:

There is only one truly philosophical problem, and that is suicide.

A. T. W. Simeons argued that the potential for suicide rests in all of us:

A tendency to self-destruction seems to be inherent in the overdeveloped human brain.

The Canadian philosopher, George P. Grant, wrote this:

When a man despairs, he does not write; he commits suicide.

Others made light of the conundrum:

To contemplate suicide is surely the best exercise of the imagination.
Phyllis Webb

Men just don't seem to jump off the bridge for big reasons; they usually do so for little ones.
W. H. Ferry

Suicide is belated acquiescence in the opinion of one's wife's relatives.
H. L. Mencken

I have had just about all I can take of myself.
S. N. Behrman

Suicide is painless; it brings on many changes.
Lyrics from the theme song for the movie, *M.A.S.H.*

From Marilyn Monroe, the words of suicide came on the phone to actor Peter Lawford, a brother-in-law of President Kennedy:

Say goodbye to Pat, say goodbye to the President, and say goodbye to yourself, because you're a nice guy.

Hollywood has endured an unusual variety of suicides, although the notes that accompany them are painfully similar:

Dearest Mummy, I am sorry, really sorry to have put you through this, but there is no way to avoid it — I love you darling, you have been the most wonderful Mum ever — and that applies to all our family. I love each and every one of them dearly. Everything goes to you — look in the files and there is a Will which decrees everything. Goodbye my Angel. Pray for me, your baby.
Carol Landis, American film-actress,
in a suicide note to her mother.

This sense of doing someone a favor by taking one's life is not limited to show business. More than a century ago Fanny Godwin, the illegitimate daughter of Mary Wollstonecraft (the mother of Mary Shelley) died with these pitiful words to her mother:

I have long determined that the best thing I could do was to put an end to the existence of a being whose birth was unfortunate and whose life has only been a series of pains to those persons who have hurt their health in endeavouring to promote her welfare. Perhaps to hear of my death may give you pain, but you will soon have the blessing of forgetting that such a creature ever existed.

Drowning was the last act of another literary woman, Virginia Woolf, whose fear of growing insane led her to write this very rational note to her husband, Leonard, then walk to the river nearby, and step in:

Virginia Woolf

Dearest,
—— I feel certain I am going mad again. I feel we can't go through another of those terrible times. And I shan't recover this time. I begin to hear voices, and I can't concentrate. So I am doing what seems the best thing to do. You have given me the greatest possible happiness. You have been in every way all that anyone could be. I don't think two people could have been happier till this terrible disease came. I can't fight any longer. I know that I am spoiling your life,

that without me you could work. And you will I know. You see, I can't even write this properly. I can't read. What I want to say is I owe all the happiness of my life to you. You have been entirely patient with me and incredibly good. I want to say that — everybody knows it. If anybody could have saved me it would have been you. Everything has gone from me but the certainty of your goodness. I can't go on spoiling your life any longer.

I don't think two people could have been happier than we have been.

V.

The poet Thomas L. Beddoes struck the usual note of apology, but not without adding a touch of wry humor:

I ought to have been among other things a good poet; Life was too great a bore on one peg and that a bad one. — Buy for Dr. Ecklin above mentioned Reade's best stomach pump.

Much more pitying was the suicide note of one Stephen Wood, the man who procured for the notorious English prostitute Christine Keeler (whose exploits brought down an entire government). Wood died from barbituate poisoning:

I am sorry I had to do this here! It's really more than I can stand — the horror day after day at the court and in the streets. It's not only fear — it's a wish not to let them get me. I'd rather get myself.

I do hope I haven't let people down too much. I tried to do my stuff, but after Marshall's summing up, I've given up all hope.

I'm sorry to disappoint the vultures — I only hope this has done the job. Delay resuscitation as long as possible.

Sylvia Plath had a history of emotional instability which had resulted in two previous suicide attempts. On February 4, 1963, she wrote to her mother:

I am going to start seeing a woman doctor, free on the National Health, to whom I've been referred by my very good local doctor, which should help me weather this difficult time. Give my love to all.

One week later she asphyxiated herself in the gas oven in her apartment.

For those outside of show business, and the literary world, suicide was a less hysterical, more rational exercise:

My wife and I choose to die in order to escape the shame of overthrow or capitulation. It is our wish for our bodies to be cremated immediately on the place where I have performed the greater part of my daily work during twelve years of service to my people.

Adolph Hitler

DER
FÜHRER
c.1945

Service? Well, if you're Adolf Hitler, service it is, which ended with those
words in his Will, recovered from the Berlin bunker where Hitler had first
poisoned his wife and then shot himself.

Hitler's generals followed suit in death, as they had done in life:

> *Everything is over. My wife and I will commit suicide. You will burn
> our bodies. Can you do that? Here is a present for you . . . .*
> Joseph Goebbels, Hitler's Minister of Propoganda.
> The present was a picture of the Führer.

You see, we shall die an honourable death.

Magda Goebbels, Joseph's wife.

I have spoken to my wife and made up my mind. I will never allow myself to be hanged by that man Hitler. I planned no murder. I only tried to serve my country, as I have done all my life. But now, this is what I must do. In about half an hour, there will come a telephone call from Ulm (his servant) to say that I have had an accident and am dead.

General Erwin Rommel.

The shame of capitulation to the Allies was matched by a different — and much more frequent — shame in the figure of Baron James Harden-Hickey, a British soldier of fortune, who discovered that his wife was living with another man. "My dear," he wrote to her from far away:

No news from you, although you have had plenty of time to write. Harvey (their son) has written to me that he has no one in view at present to buy my land. Well, I shall have tasted the cup of bitterness to the very dreggs, but I do not complain. Goodbye. I forgive you your conduct towards me and trust that you will be able to forgive yourself. I prefer to be a dead gentleman to a living blackguard like your father.

Only a few practitioners of the final act were able to bring some humor to the falling curtain. Hart Crane, the American poet, jumped overboard following an uproarious cruise-ship party, yelling back:

Goodbye everybody!

The English speculator, Barney Barnato, also jumped overboard and threw back a question:

What's the time?

The final testament of Ureli Corelli Hill, founder of the New York Philharmonic Society, was a joking revenge:

Ha, Ha, I go! The sooner the better!

It was echoed by Joseph Duveen, art dealer to the wealthy, who left just in time:

Well, I fooled 'em for five years.

And when Henry Ward Beecher, an American clergyman, was asked by his doctor how high he could raise his arm he replied:

Well, high enough to hit you, doctor!

For George Eastman, inventor of the Kodak camera, suicide was simply an acceleration of nature:

To my friends: My work is done. Why wait? G. E.

Shakespeare was a master of the language of suicide, revealing many subtle differences in this common theme. When Othello, the black moor, killed himself, he had a long word with his murderer before the end:

Soft you; a word or two before you go.
I have done the state some service, and they know't.
No more of that. I pray you, in your letters,
When you shall these unlucky deeds relate,
Speak of me as I am; nothing extenuate,
Nor set down aught in malice. Then must you speak
Of one that lov'd not wisely, but too well.
Of one not easily jealous, but being wrought
Perplex'd in the extreme; of one whose hand,
Like the base Indian, threw a pearl away
Richer than all his tribe; of one whose subdu'd eyes,
Drop tears as fast as the Arabian trees
Their medicinal gum. Set you down this;
And say besides, that in Aleppo once,
Where a malignant and a turban'd Turk
Beat a Venetian and traduc'd the state,
I took by the throat the circumcised dog,
And smote him thus — [stabs himself]

The final words on the final act, however, belongs to the American satirist Dorothy Parker. This poem, published in *Enough Rope,* gives an exceedingly practical reason for hanging around:

RESUMÉ

Razors pain you,
Rivers are damp.
Acids stain you,
And drugs cause a cramp.
Guns aren't lawful;
Nooses give;
Gas smells awful;
You might as well live.

If suicide is the slow, carefully thought-out decision to do away with oneself, assassination is just the opposite for the victim, though just the same for the assassin. Benjamin Disraeli was surely wrong when he said that:

Assassination has never changed the history of the world.

But these words were hardly uttered before murder became a legitimate arm of far too many foreign policies. The United States has shown that it too has a constitution based on democracy, moderated by assassination.

The madness of the 1960's brought the most terrible series of assassinations in America's history. President John Kennedy died in silence in Dallas, and one day later, his accused assassin, Lee Harvey Oswald, was gunned down. Six minutes before the shots, Oswald said this to the Secret Service:

> *I will be glad to discuss this proposition with my attorney, and that after I talk with one, we could either discuss it with him, or discuss it with my attorney, if the attorney thinks it is a wise thing to do, but at the present time, I have nothing to say to you.*

Five years later in Los Angeles, Bobby Kennedy was shot by Sirhan Sirhan, minutes after becoming the front-runner for the Democratic Presidential nomination. His last choking gasp was:

> *Oh no, oh no . . . don't lift me, don't lift me.*

Almost two thousand years earlier, Julius Caesar was stabbed to death on the steps of the Roman senate, uttering the most famous dying words of all:

> *Et tu, Brute?*

Brutus' guilt-fed melancholy over his participation in Caesar's death culminated in sharp hallucinations which took the form of the dead Caesar. Unable to bear such persecution, Brutus took his own life. His last words, according to Shakespeare, were:

> *Caesar, now be still;*
> *I killed not thee with half so good a will.*

Occasionally, assassination brings out the best — in the worst of us:

> *Who is there?*
>
> Billy the Kid, answering the knock on his door.
>
> *You've got me, boys. I've had enough.*
>
> The dying whisper of Red Ryan,
> notorious Canadian bank robber,
> after a shoot-out with police.

Assassination came to Canada in 1970, taking with it Pierre Laporte, a Quebec Cabinet Minister kidnapped by members of the radical Front de Libération du Québec (FLQ) Party. While in their hands, Laporte wrote this letter to his colleague, Premier Robert Bourassa:

> *My Dear Robert: You have the power to dispose of my life. . . . I am convinced that I am writing the most important letter of my life.*

A few days later, Laporte was found dead in the trunk of an abandoned car.

In the Middle East, where death has become a way of life, a United Nations mediator paused to inspect the bullet hole in the wheel of his automobile prior to beginning a journey. When a journalist shouted "Good luck!" the officer called back . . .

Thanks. I'll need it!

. . . and drove on. An hour later he was found shot by unknown assassins.

The brevity of these final words reveals one of the minor problems of dying suddenly and violently. The unexpectedness of it all conspires against leisurely loquation. Much more fruitful for the student of studied farewells is the execution, accompanied in most civilized countries by the opportunity for the condemned to sum up their lives for the last time — and occasionally to summon up their redemption.

The mood of the soon-to-be deceased has varied, from pride:

> *It is no shame to stand on this scaffold. I served my Fatherland as others before me.*
>
> General Karl Brandt, Hitler's personal surgeon,
> as the hood was put over his face.

. . . to expectation:

> *I am coming, Katie.*
>
> Major Herbert Rowse Armstrong, executed
> for poisoning his wife, Katie.

. . . to fiery defiance:

> *Oh ye Papists! Behold ye look for miracles and here now you may see a miracle; For in this fire, I feel no more pain, than if I were in a bed of down, but it is to me as a bed of roses.*
>
> James Bainham, Protestant martyr burned at the
> stake.

. . . to impatience:

> *Don't keep me waiting any longer than necessary.*
>
> John Brown, on the scaffold.

Modesty is a quality uncommon to the execution stand, but when the sister of Louis XVI, Madame Elizabeth, was guillotined, she fell on the scaffold before her turn and, with her blouse flying up above her, pleaded with the executioner:

> *In the name of your mother, monsieur, cover me.*

Her brother faced the blade a shade more defiantly, addressing the crowd:

> *Frenchmen! I die guiltless of the crimes imputed to me. Pray God my blood not fall on France. It so . . .*
>
> Louis XVI of France

Not so for Bonnie Brown Hardy, whose modesty overcame her as she sat strapped in the electric chair, asking:

> *Is my dress pulled down?*

Occasionally, the end comes before the final sentence is completed. The Irish nationalist, Robert Emmet, was asked by the hangman if he was ready. Emmet replied:

Not . . .

and the trap door opened.

A similar experience befell Neil Cream, an English murderer, who blurted out:

I am Jack . . .

before the noose took hold. His enigmatic goodbye has led some sleuths to speculate that Cream was the notorious Jack the Ripper.

The French Revolution brought out the good humor in no one, although one revolutionist, Jean François Ducos, faced the block with admirable *sang-froid:*

It is time the Convention decreed the inviolability of heads.

Jean Sylvain Bailly, guillotined in the French Revolution, answered his executioner's taunt, "You are trembling, Bailly," with an icy rebuff:

My friend, I am cold, and will soon be cold forever.

Sir Thomas More met his Maker via the axe, but not before he had told his executioner:

Pluck up thy spirits, man, and be not afraid to do thine office. My neck is very short; take heed, therefore, thou strike not awry, for saving of thy honesty.

Moments before, More addressed his guard as he ascended the scaffold to die for the crime of treason against Henry VIII:

I pray you, Master Lieutenant, see me safe up, and for my coming down, let me shift for myself.

In the dramatized version of More's life and death, Robert Bolt's *A Man For All Seasons,* he had this to say on the subject of his demise:

Friend, be not afraid of your office. You send me to God. He will not refuse one who is so blithe to go to Him.

The Scottish pirate, Captain William Kidd, blamed almost everyone for his fate:

This is a very fickle and faithless generation.

For the Russian Revolutionary, Bestoujeff, the final act was indicative of what brought him to the noose in the first place. After the hangman's rope accidentally broke as he was on the way down, Bestoujeff despaired:

Nothing succeeds with me. Even here I meet with disappointment.

Joseph Barnave, an apostate of Jacobinism, clearly thought his countrymen ungrateful; at his execution he stamped his foot on the scaffold, saying:

This then is my reward?

And John of Barneveld, a champion of Dutch independence, sought only a fast end to what he saw as a great embarrassment. To his executioner he said:

Be quick about it, be quick.

For an American armed robber who faced the firing squad in Utah at the turn of the century, there was one final — and highly insulting request:

Bury me somewhere else. I don't want to be found dead in Utah.

However, at least two other men seem to have had a keen desire to be found dead in Utah. In 1960, James W. Rodgers was executed for murder. When asked if he had a last request, he smilingly said:

Why, yes — a bullet proof vest.

On January 17, 1978, a convicted murderer named Gary Gilmour faced another Utah firing squad, ending the ten-year suspension of capital punishment in the United States. It was the final act in a bizarre drama that combined attempted suicide with a fatal desire to be shot. Gilmour wanted only "to die like a man," and when his lawyers insisted on launching appeals for a stay of execution their client told them to forget it. Before hundreds of journalists from around the world, Gilmour requested that he die bare-headed and standing up. This was refused by warden Sam Smith. So his head was covered with a hood and he was strapped to a wooden chair twenty-five feet away from five hidden marksmen. Gilmour's final words were:

Let's do it!

Gilmour's seeming disdain for death has been matched by men of similar composure:

Keep cool, Warden. Take your time.
Willie Kemmler, the first man to be executed
in the electric chair, 1890.

It will be but a momentary pang.
John André, an English officer
on the scaffold, 1780.

Pound, pound the pouch containing Anaxarchus; ye pound not Anaxarchus.
The Greek philosopher, who was pounded
to death with pestles.

Take this wine. You must need some in your profession. It is finished, gentlemen. I leave for the great voyage.
Duc de Biron, who was eating oysters and drinking
wine with friends in prison before the executioner came.

Women, it seems, swagger less in the presence of death. Ruth Snyder killed her husband in 1928 and, as she was strapped into the electric chair, she cried out:

Jesus have mercy on me. I have sinned.

Mary Blandy, whose lover induced her to poison her father in 1751, wept at the scaffold:

Gentlemen, don't hang me high for the sake of decency.... I'm afraid I shall fall.

Two Archbishops of Canterbury were put to death by their monarchs, William Laud in 1645, and Thomas Cranmer in 1556. Cranmer was burned at the stake and, as the flames rose about him, he thrust his hand in first, the hand that had signed his religious conversion:

This hand having sinned in signing the writing must be the first to suffer punishment! This hand hath offended....

Laud, on the other hand, was beheaded with great anticipation:

Lord, I am coming as fast as I can. I know I must pass through the shadow of death before I come to Thee. But it is a mere shadow of death, a little darkness upon nature....

The most stirring of all last words belongs properly to Socrates, who was sentenced to death by the Athenian court for impiety and corrupting the youth of Athens. His famous essay, *On His Condemnation to Death,* shows that philosophy lives, even in death:

But it is now time to depart, for me to die, for you to live. But which of us is going to a better state is unknown to everyone but God.

Yet the most famous last words of execution belong to the American patriot, Nathan Hale:

I regret that I have but one life to lose for my country....

Hale's pride was counterpointed by the words of America's most infamous traitor, Benedict Arnold, who seemed more concerned with regret and dress than death:

Let me die in the old uniform in which I fought my battles for freedom. May God forgive me for putting on any other.

... and in equal measure by American's most famous assassin, John Wilkes Booth, who murdered Abraham Lincoln:

Tell my mother that I died for my country. . . . I thought I did for the best. . . . Useless! Useless!

One of the most notorious executions in modern times belonged to Nicola Sacco and Bartolomeo Vanzetti, Italian immigrants to Boston, who were convicted of murdering a paymaster and a guard during a robbery in 1923. They were considered anarchists as well, and their hanging on August 23, 1927, was met with mass protests abroad. Both proclaimed their innocence to the end, and met their Maker with these words:

Vive il Anarchismo! . . . Farewell my wife and child and all my friends! Good . . . good evening, gentlemen. . . . Addio, mamma mia, addio, mamma mia.

Nicola Sacco

I want to thank you. I want to thank you for everything you have done for me, warden. . . . I wish to tell you, all of you, that I am innocent. I have never done a crime. Maybe, oh yes, maybe sometimes I have done some sin, but not a crime. I am innocent of all crime, not only of this, but of all, of all. I am an innocent man. . . . I wish to forgive some people for what they are now doing to me.

Bartolomeo Vanzetti

The execution of Ethel and Julius Rosenberg for alledgedly transmitting U.S. atomic secrets to the Russians was also met with anti-American protests at home and abroad. Their farewell to each other began immediately after their sentencing in what is remembered as the greatest political trial of their generation. Mrs. Rosenberg, who once studied voice, turned to her husband and sang *One Fine Day,* from the opera *Madame Butterfly,* and the popular song, *Goodnight Irene.* Her husband returned the compliment by singing *The Battle Hymn of the Republic.*

On their day of execution, June 19, 1953, Julius Rosenberg said farewell to his wife by touching the tips of his fingers to hers through the wire mesh of the holding room. The executioner had to give Ethel five shots of 2,000 volts each before she was pronounced dead. Said *The New York Times:*

They went to their deaths with a composure that astonished the witnesses.

Chapter 7

"Woe is me. Methinks I'm turning into a god."
Roman Emperor Suetonius

Perhaps it is because death is their business that many military men have died with a modicum of eloquence or posterity on their lips. Lord Horatio Nelson, who admonished his sailors that "now is the time for all good men to come to the aid of their country," died at Trafalgar as he had lived:

Thank God I have done my duty.

Lafayette, the French soldier and statesman, was more sanguine on his deathbed...

What do you expect? Life is like the flame of a lamp; when there is no more oil — zest! It goes out and it is all over.

...while Napoleon was more hysterical, leaving us forever with this strange farewell:

France! Army! Head of the Army! Josephine!

From Ethan Allen, American Revolutionary soldier, came grim defiance in the face of death. In answer to his doctor, who warned:

General, I fear the Angels are waiting for you,

Allen replied:

Waiting, are they? Waiting, are they?! Well, let 'em wait!

The Confederate General "Stonewall" Jackson was considerably more relaxed when he died, whispering to his aides:

Let us go over, and sit in the shade of the trees.

With complete resignation George C. Atcheson, an aide to General MacArthur, saw that the plane carrying himself and twelve others was going to crash in the Pacific, and said:

Well, it can't be helped.

Crowfoot, the Blackfoot Indian Chief, flew first into poetry and then into heaven:

A little while and I will be gone from among you, whither I cannot tell. From nowhere we came, into nowhere we go. What is life? It is a flash of a firefly in the night. It is a breath of a buffalo in the winter-time. It is as the little shadow that runs across the grass and loses itself in the sunset.

Indians were a particular thorn to the American General George Custer, especially after he met them at the Battle of Little Big Horn, otherwise known as Custer's Last Stand. As Custer approached certain death, he said to his Indian scout named "Goes Ahead":

My scout, if we win the battle, you will be one of the noted men in the Crow Nation. . . . I have forgotten to tell you, you are not to fight in this battle, but to go back and save your life.

"Goes Ahead" did save his life, and wrote a book about the slaughter of the white armies called *The Vanishing Race,* in which he said:

If we had been smart, we would have asked General Custer for a recommendation beforehand. But we did not know much in those days.

Three other Indians who survived the battle were ready to die, and made that clear to their warriors:

Come on children. Do not be scared.

Chief Two Moons

Only heaven and earth last long. Hokay, hey brother! My life will not last forever.

Chief Joseph White Bull

But I kept going and shouting, 'It's a good day to die!' so that everyone who heard would know I was not afraid of being killed in battle.

Dewey Beard, warrior.

Such sentiments are lovely, but not quite suitable for the likes of Confederate General Lewis Armistead, who died at the Battle of Gettysburg with this command:

Give them the cold steel, boys!

Yet the most famous military goodbye belongs to the British, who, at the Battle of Balaclava in 1852, sent 670 untrained cavalrymen on an attack against 3,000 Russian cavalry. Three hundred members of the Light Brigade were slaughtered. Today, only the glory remains in Alfred Tennyson's stirring defense of the British Empire, *The Charge of the Light Brigade:*

Half a league, half a league,
Half a league onward,
All in the valley of Death
Rode the six hundred.
"Forward, the Light Brigade!
Charge for the guns!" he said:
Into the valley of Death
Rode the six hundred.

The destruction of Hiroshima by American forces in W.W. II marked a goodbye to the non-nuclear age and ushered in a new threat to world peace that is still with us today. More human beings died at one time during the bombing of Hiroshima than in any other single military man-oeuvre, and writer Robert Schwartz brings a peculiar view of the holocaust — from the man who dropped the first atom bomb:

> *Back at the right waist window, Sgt. Bob Shumrd, the assistant flight engineer, turned his polaroids (binoculars) to full intensity and prepared to take advantage of the fact that he had the best seat for the show.... He adjusted his polaroids to mild intensity and looked down at Hiroshima. A large white cloud was spreading rapidly over the whole area, obscuring everything, and rising very rapidly.*

But if war brings out the most brutal sentiments, religion exists in part to reveal the most agonizingly beautiful. Of all the farewells known to man, this is easily the most significant, and the one over which immeasureable blood has been shed:

> *And they brought him to the place named Golgotha (which means the place of the skull). And they offered him wine mingled with myrrh; but he did not take it. And they crucified him, and divided his garments among them, casting lots for them, to decide what each should take. And it was the third hour when they crucified him. And the inscription of the charge against him read, "The King of the Jews." ... And when the sixth hour had come, there was darkness over the whole land until the ninth hour. And at the ninth hour Jesus cried with a loud voice, "E'lo-i, E'lo-i, la'ma sabach-tha'ni?" which means, "My God, my God, why hast thou forsaken me?" And some of the bystanders hearing it said, "Behold, he is calling Eli'jah." And one ran and, filling a sponge full of vinegar, put it on a reed and gave it to him to drink, saying, "Wait, let us see whether Eli'jah will come to take him down." And Jesus uttered a loud cry and breathed his last. And the curtain of the temple was torn in two, from top to bottom. And when the centurion, who stood facing him, saw that he thus breathed his last, he said, "Truly this man was a son of God!"*
> *The Gospel according to Mark,* 15: 22-39

Religion casts a hopeful shadow over death, as visions of the hereafter mix with thoughts of what has been into a confusion of what might be:

Now comes the mystery.

Henry Ward Beecher, American clergyman.

It is another thing to die than people have imagined.

St. Boniface, as boiling lead was poured
into his mouth.

Oh dear, dear, dear me! We are dead.

Rev. John Bumby, clinging to a canoe
in a frigid river.

I have sent for you that you may see how a Christian can die.

Joseph Addison to his stepson.

For Martin Luther, the final world came as his diseased heart failed and he lost consciousness and died with his friends shouting questions into his deaf ears. They wanted to know whether his faith in Christ remained steadfast as he approached the end. His answer:

Yes.

Saint Laurence, who was boiled alive on a gridiron, had this to say on the spit:

This side is now roasted enough. Turn up, O tyrant great; assay whether roasted or raw this thinkest the better meat.

Such fiery humor was alive and well with the Roman Emperor Suetonius, who, like all Roman Emperors, was thought to be deified after death. The logic of his last words is as irrefutable as their economy:

Woe is me. Me thinks I'm turning into a god.

Religion itself can strike back with a vengeance. Condemned to death for having mutilated a crucifix, Jean François le Fevre said ingenuously:

I did not think they would put a young man to death for such a trifle.

When Heinrich Heine, the German poet, was told on his deathbed that God would forgive him his sins, Heine was more than pragmatic, saying:

Why, of course He will forgive me; that's His business.

Listening to the American clergyman, Cotton Mather, one is tempted to think that Heine is right:

Is this dying? Is this all? Is this what I feared when I prayed against a hard death? I can bear this! I can bear it!!

If confrontations with the Almighty can lead to such revelations by our holy representatives, similar close encounters by men and women of song and dance suggest that the show must go on:

> *Curtain! Fast music! Lights!! Ready for the last finale! Great. The show looks good! The show looks good!*
>> Florenz Ziegfeld, American theatrical producer.

> *Get my Swan costume ready.*
>> The last words of Anna Pavlova,
>> the Russian ballerina, in a delirium of fever.

> *Adieu, my friends! I go to glory!*
>> Isadora Duncan

Guy Lombardo, bandleader and introducer of many New Year celebrations, said this about his own death:

> *I'll be standing on a bandstand 'till I die. Hopefully, it will be when they're ringing in the year 1993, and I'll be standing up there leading them in Auld Lang Syne, while everybody's dancing and having a ball.*

Lombardo died in 1977.

Enrico Caruso, the renowned operatic tenor, died with irony on his lips:

> *Doro, I can't get my breath.*

Beethoven, who was stone deaf, hollered out:

> *Too bad! Too bad!! It's too late!*

when the wine he asked for arrived; Beethoven promptly died.

Occasionally, death is just another insult:

> *It is said . . . that Liszt got Verdi to give him a letter of introduction to Rossini and went to call on him. Rossini was exceedingly polite, and asked him to play, and when he had done, inquired what the piece was.*

> *Liszt said: 'It is a march I have written on the death of Meyerbeer. How do you like it, Maestro?'*

> *Rossini said he liked it very much, but added as he bade farewell to his guest: 'Do you not think it would have been better if it had been you who had died and Meyerbeer who had written the music?'*

W. S. Gilbert, the first half of Gilbert and Sullivan, leaped into a river to rescue a woman from drowning, only to find that she was drowning him. His last words before going down for the last time were:

> *Put your hands on my shoulders and don't struggle.*

Rufus Griswold, a literary executor, died like a gentleman:

> *Sir, I may not have been always a Christian, but I am very sure that I have been a gentleman.*

Lady Mary Wortley Montagu, died with indifference:

It's all been very interesting.

while actor Douglas Fairbanks said:

I never felt better.

and Adam Short, a Canadian economist, died logically:

Oh, a man's got to die of something!

There are some goodbyes that defy classification, and while they are deserving of preservation they are not the sort of thing you are likely to quote at parties. We have included them in *The Goodbye Book* because, in a special way, each represents a fall from innocence and a farewell to a way of life.

One of the most eccentric defences of human life and farewells to law and order, took place in a small Missouri town when George Graham Vest, a lawyer and U.S. Senator, was retained by a client who was suing another man for killing his dog. During the trial, Vest showed no interest at all in the testimony, but won the case when he rose to address the jury with these words:

> *If fortune drives the master forth an outcast into the world, friendless and homeless, the faithful dog asks no higher privilege than that of accompanying him to guard against danger, to fight against his enemies.*

> *And when the last scene of all comes and death takes his master in its embrace and his body is laid away on the cold ground, no matter if all other friends pursue their way, there by the graveside will be the noble dog be found, his head between his paws, his eyes sad, but open in alert watchfullness, faithful and true even in death.*

Though Vest was speaking of dogs, even his fertile imagination failed to match the notorious Charles Manson for the strangeness of the subject matter, or peculiarity of the appeal. Manson was convicted of killing actress Sharon Tate in 1971. One of Manson's many accomplices was Susan Atkins, who said after stabbing Miss Tate:

> *You have to have a real love in your heart to do this for people.*

Manson himself did nothing to refute the belief that he was insane. In a statement issued after his conviction, Manson said:

> *Mr. and Mrs. America — you are wrong. I am not the King of the Jews nor am I a hippie cult leader. I am what you have made of me, and the mad dog, devil, killer, friend, leper is a reflection of your society. . . . Whatever the outcome of this madness that you call a fair trial or Christian justice, you know this: In my mind's eye, my thoughts light fire in your cities.*

For courtroom oratory of a much different style, we turn to Patrick Henry, a leader of the American Revolution, who delivered this impassioned speech in 1775:

> *Is life so dear, or peace so sweet, as to be purchased at the price of chains and slavery? Forbid it, Almighty God! I know not what course others may take; but as for me, give me liberty or give me death.*

Edward Everett, another American orator, took a highly optimistic view of his condition. In a letter to his daughter, he said:

> *I have turned the corner, and as soon as I can get a little appetite, shake off my carking cough, and get the kidneys to resume their action, and subdue the numbness in my limbs, and get the better of the neuralgic pain in the left shoulder, I hope to do nicely.*

These proved to be his last words.

Henry Fox, on the other hand, was not so magnanimous. When his arch-enemy, George Augustus Selwyn, asked to see him for one last time, Fox announced:

> *If Mr. Selwyn calls, let him in; if I am alive, I shall be very glad to see him, and if I am dead, he shall be very glad to see me.*

A similar lack of illusion greeted the American aviator Amelia Earhart. In a letter to her husband, written before what turned out to be her last flight, she said:

> *Please know that I am quite aware of the hazards. I want to do it because I want to do it. Women must try to do things as men have tried. When they fail, their failure must be but a challenge to others.*

But if Miss Earhart was gentle in dispensing blame, Matthew B. Begbie most certainly was not. In 1898, the "hanging judge" of British Columbia said this to the accused after the jury had declared a sentence of life imprisonment rather than the death sentence:

> *It is not a pleasant duty for me to have to sentence you only to prison for life; your crime was unmitigated murder, you deserve to be hanged. Had the jury done their duty, I might now have the painful satisfaction of condemning you to death. . . .*

He then turned his anger on the jury:

> *. . . You, gentlemen of the jury, permit me to say that it would give me great pleasure to see you hanged, each and every one of you, for bringing in a murderer guilty only of manslaughter.*

The judge's vituperation was matched by that of Camille Benoit Desmoulins, who, in a speech before the French Parliament in 1793, called for the execution of Louis XVI:

> *. . . he paid his bodyguard at Coblentz and betrayed the nation. And it only remains for you to prove, as Brutus proved to the Roman people, that you are worthy to begin the Republic and its Constitution, and to appease the shades of a hundred thousand citizens whom he caused to perish in pronouncing the same sentence: 'Go Lictor, bind him to the stake'.*

Such rough justice did not die with the French Revolution. The Iranian Revolution of 1979 saw members of the dreaded secret police, SAVAK, tried in secret and sentenced *en masse* to death. The following exchange took place between Major Bijan Yahyaki and the chief of the revolutionary court:

MAJOR: *The system was there. I didn't create*
anything.

COURT: *This is not a personal matter. You are*
standing in front of the Iranian nation,
which was tortured. You made the traitorous
Shah, the Shah of the country. Islam never
gave you the right to do this.

MAJOR: *I was forced. Put yourself in my place.*
You wouldn't understand it unless you put
yourself in my shoes. I asked for the transfer.
I tried hard to get out. You must take that
into consideration.

COURT: *Come on. Your crime is not being a prison*
guard, your crime is stepping on the human
rights of people.

MAJOR: *I'm a nobody. I wasn't important in the system.*
If I was a somebody, I wouldn't have this job.

Five minutes later, the major was sentenced to be shot by a firing squad.

The true lasting value of a final goodbye is often highest when the person uttering it is the neighborhood of heaven. That is why the final farewells of monarchs, dictators, and other representatives of heaven on earth are still with us centuries after they have gone.

Noblesse oblige was a characteristic of kingly death:

> *Gentlemen, I am sorry for keeping you working like this — I am*
> *unable to concentrate.*
>
> George V

> *I have been an unconscionable time dying . . . I hope that you will*
> *excuse it.*
>
> Charles II

Henry VIII was less forgiving of human frailty, especially when it concerned wives, all six of whom either died during his office or were executed by him:

CATHERINE HOWARD:
> *(who died referring to Thomas Culpepper, one of her many lovers)*
> *I die a Queen, but I would rather die the wife*
> *of Culpepper. . . . God have mercy on my soul.*

LADY JANE GREY:
> *(who blindfolded herself and could not find
> the execution block)*
>
> *What shall I do? Where is it?*

Anne Boleyn spoke out boldly to the crowd that in minutes would see her head roll:

> *Good Christian people, I am come hither to die, for according to the law and by the law I am judged to die, and therefore I will speak nothing against it. I am come hither to accuse no man, nor to speak anything of what whereof I am accused and condemned to die.*

Without a tremor, her voice continued:

> *But I pray God save the King and send him long to reign over you. For a gentler nor a more merciful prince was there never: and to me he was ever a good, a gentle, and sovereign lord. And if any person will meddle in my cause I require them to judge the best. And thus I take leave of the world and pray for you all, and I heartily desire you all to pray for me.*

One of her ladies-in-waiting tied a piece of linen around her eyes as she approached the block. Anne bowed her head, and gave the signal to the executioner:

> *To Christ I commend my soul, Jesu, receive my soul, To Christ. . . .*

Tradition has it that after her head rolled, her eyes and lips went on moving for awhile.

Other kings and queens went out with few words, though similar thoughts:

> *Why do you weep. Did you think I was immortal?*
> > Louis XIV, the Sun King.

> *Farewell, my children, forever. I go to your Father.*
> > Marie Antoinette, Louis' wife.

> *I am a Queen, but I have not the power to move my arms.*
> > Louise of Russia

> *Oh, God, I am dying. This is death.*
> > George IV

ANNE BOLEYN

The King's death is moving peacefully towards its close.
Medical notice on the condition of George V.

No, I shall go on; I shall work to the end.
Edward VII

Remember, I go from a corruptible to an incorruptible crown, where no disturbance can be, but peace and joy for evermore.
Charles I

A King should die standing.
Louis XVIII

Ay Jesus.
Charles V

Epitaphs

Every life, and every book, deserves a final comment. For those people who fail to make it into the next life after leaving this one, there is always the consolation prize of rewriting history in your epitaph. The art of tombstone writing has filled graveyards with prose (and poetry) like this:

To follow you
I am not content.
How do I know
Which way you went?

In a Waynesville, North Carolina cemetery.

School is out
Teacher has gone home.

Professor S. B. McCracken's epitaph
in an Elkhart, Indiana cemetery.

I told you I was sick.

In a Georgia cemetery.

Here lies
Ezekial Akile
Age 102
The Good
Die Young.

In a Nova Scotia cemetery.

Once I wasn't
Then I was
Now I ain't again.

Arthur C. Homan's epitaph
in an Ohio cemetery.

Gone, but not forgiven.

Written by a widow on her adulterous ,
husband's gravestone in an Atlanta cemetery.

If those strike you as refreshing examples of the truth, Otto von Bismark would disagree. His dying words were:

I do not want a lying official epitaph. Write on my tomb that I was the faithful servant of my master, the Emperor Willam, King of Prussia.

Canadians, it seems, like to make sure that those who survive them are given the most polished, professional epitaph to ponder. These last words, written while the authors are still alive, are a milder form of life insurance:

Here lies the body of Harold E. Ballard,
Who didn't do anything bad,
And didn't do anything good.
Lived by the golden rule
And doesn't care where he goes,
Because he'll have friends in both places.

Harold Ballard, sports impresario, 1979.

If you think THAT was something,
Stay tuned for the SECOND act.

Al Waxman, TV Star, 1979.

Here lies Craig Russell, who finally got laid
with the rest of them.
He died broke,
Exploited and cheated by crooked producers and
promoters.
Always at his best on a full moon,
Craig filled the promise to always leave them
laughing. Buried in drag, she will be missed.

Craig Russell, female impersonator, 1979.

The English poet Samuel Taylor Coleridge met death with the genius of his life in this Epitaph, written eight months before he passed away:

EPITAPH
Stop, Christian passer by! Stop, child of God,
And read with gentle breast. Beneath this sod
A poet lies, or that which once seemed he.

O, lift one thought in prayer for S.T.C.;
That he who many a year with toil of breath
Found death in life, may here find life in death!
Mercy for praise — to be forgiven for fame
He asked, and hoped, through Christ. Do thou the same.

Samuel Taylor Coleridge

Others passed less poetically:

Born a man. Died a grocer.

Epitaph of John Smith in a
New Brunswick cemetery.

He called
Bill Smith
A liar.

In a Cripple Creek, Colorado cemetary.

In memory of Robert Randall, Esq., M.P.P.,
The victim of Colonial Misrule, who died May 21, 1831,
age 68 years.

Epitaph of the reformer who tried in vain
to redress the personal injustices
done to him. This inscription is in
the Drummond Hill Cemetery, Niagara Falls.

Sir John Strange
Here lies an honest lawyer,
and that is Strange.

A lawyer's epitaph in England.

The opportunity to add our own epitaph to this collection of fond farewells has proven to be irresistable. And so, borrowing from Winston Churchill, we end *The Goodbye Book* with:

The Goodbye Glossary

Everybody has somebody they want to say goodbye to — a mother-in-law, a good friend, a lover, a bill collector — but in the end it seems we all get the goodbyes we deserve. The following list of contemporary ways to say goodbye, although far from complete, is meant to be an entertaining addendum to your own repertoire of "50 ways to leave your lover."

à bientôt
à demain
a rivederci
addio
adieu
adios
all aboard
all good things
allons-y, Alonzo
aloha
au revoir
auf Wiedersehen
avaunt
away with you

be off
be seeing you
beat it
begone
bon voyage
bye bye
bye for now
bung-ho
buzz off

call me some time
catch you later
cheerio
chin-chin
ciao-ciao, cheri
clear out

don't call us, we'll call you
drop dead

excuse me
exit stage left

fare thee well
farewell

get out
get out of my life
get lost
go
go about your business
go fly a kite
go jump in a lake
go soak your head
god bless
goodbye
goodbye, Charlie
good night
good night, Chet; good night, David
good riddance
good talking to you
gotta go

hang in there
happy trails
hasta la vista
have a good day (hagady)
have a good time

have a nice day (H.A.N.D.)
here's your hat, what's your
   hurry
hi ho Silver and away
hit the road
hop it
I never want to see you again
I quit
I think you'd better go now
I want to be alone
If I don't see you in the future,
   I'll see you in the pasture
I'll call you
I'll let you go now
I'm gettin' out of here
I'm taking the first train out of
   town
I'm through
I'm walking
It's been a slice
It's been nice
It's over
It's too late

let's blow this popsicle stand
let's slide

make like a banana and split
make like a tree and leaf
may all your enemies drop at
   your feet
may the force be with you
may the wind always be at your
   back

nice seeing you

off with you

peace
pip-pip

salut
sayonara
scoot
scram
see ya
see you later, alligator; in a
   while, crocodile

see you tomorrow
shalom
shoo
shove off
shuffle off to Buffalo
shut the door on your way out
so long
stay healthy

take a powder
take care
take it easy
take off
ta-ta for now (T.T.F.N.)
ten-four
thank you
thanks for calling
thanks for stopping by
the end is near, the end is here
'till next time
tinkety-tink
toodle-oo

until we meet again

vamoose

we'll talk
we're through

you're fired

Index of Personal Names

Acknowledgements

The authors wish to thank Barbara Shainbaum and Ellen Kates, whose research skills made this task more pleasurable.

Permission to use copyright material is gratefully acknowledged to the following:

Hogarth Press for a letter from *Virginia Woolf: A Biography* by Quentin Bell; United Artists Corporation for an extract from *Last Tango in Paris* by Bernardo Bertolucci; John Murray Ltd. for a letter from *Byron: A Self Portrait* ed. by Peter Quennell; *Canadian Magazine* for three epitaphs; Jonathan Cape for two letters from *Carrington: Letters and Extracts from her Diary* ed. by David Garnett; Weidenfeld and Nicolson Limited for extracts from *Love Letters: An Anthology* by Antonia Fraser, and for an extract from *Tussy is Me* by Michael Hastings; Charles Scribner's Sons for extracts from *A Farewell to Arms* and *The Sun Also Rises* by Ernest Hemingway; the Society of Authors for the Estate of A.E. Housman for 'Because I Liked You Better' from *Collected Poems* by A.E. Housman; Chatto and Windus for an extract from *Texts and Pretexts* by Aldous Huxley; Random House Inc. for an extract from *A Doll's House* by Henrik Ibsen, reprinted in *Six Plays by Henrik Ibsen,* trans. by Eva Le Gallienne; Cassell & Company Ltd. for an extract from *Flowers for Algernon* by Daniel Keyes; J.M. Dent & Sons Ltd. and Methuen & Company Ltd. for a letter from *The Letters of Charles Lamb* ed. by E.V. Lucas; George Allen & Unwin Ltd. for 'Goodbye' from *Ha, Ha, Among the Trumpets* by Alun Lewis; Gerald Duckworth and Co. Ltd for 'The Terrible Door' from *Harold Monro:*

Collected Poems by Harold Monro; William Collins Sons and Co. Ltd. for a letter from *Harold Nicolson: Diaries and Letters* ed. by Nigel Nicolson; The Viking Press for two poems from *The Portable Dorothy Parker* by Dorothy Parker; William Morrow and Co. for extracts from *Peter's Quotations* by Laurence J. Peter; Harper & Row Publishers, Inc. for a letter from *Letters Home* by Sylvia Plath, ed. by A.S. Plath; André Deutsch Ltd. for an extract from *Voyage in the Dark* by Jean Rhys; Houghton Mifflin Co. Ltd. for an extract from *Goodbye, Columbus* by Philip Roth; Pitman Publishing Ltd. for a letter from *Intimate Letters of England's Queens* by Margaret Saunders; Simon and Schuster for letters from *A Treasury of the World's Greatest Letters* and *A Second Treasury of the World's Greatest Letters* ed. by Lincoln M. Schuster; Oxford University Press for a letter from *The Letters of Laurence Sterne* ed. by Lewis Perry Curtis; Dodd, Mead & Co. Ltd. for extracts from *The Home Book of Quotations* by Burton Stevenson; Oxford University Press for a letter from *The Correspondence of Jonathan Swift* ed. by Harold Williams; Lorrimer Publishing Ltd. for an extract from *Jules and Jim* by François Truffaut, translation Copyright © 1968 by Lorrimer Publishing Ltd.; Cassell & Company Ltd. for extracts from *Love Letters: An Anthology from the British Isles* ed. by James Turner.

Although every effort has been made to ensure that permissions for all material were obtained, those sources not formally acknowledged here will be included in all future editions of this book.

My Goodbye Diary

Not everybody wants to go to the grave to get their parting words immortalized. Here's a chance for you to record your own moments of glory, victory, passion and panache.

The authors invite you to contribute your own favorite goodbye scenes to subsequent editions of this book.